# Reinvigorating Classroom Climate

*Reinvigorating Classroom Climate* offers educators practical, reliable guidance for fostering more inspiring environments. Teachers and students alike need to show up to school feeling like they have a sense of purpose and will be welcomed, cared for, and nourished. Full of immediately actionable mini-solutions, this book gives frontline educators the everyday tools they need to establish the conditions that support positive mindsets, relationship-building, and social-emotional learning. These strategies cover it all: motivation and engagement, human dignity and purpose, moral and character development, bullying and absence, and much more. School teachers, teacher leaders, student support staff, and other K-12 professionals will come away with a wealth of action steps designed to fit into and enhance, rather than replace, their existing learning culture and climate.

**Maurice J. Elias** is Professor of Psychology, Director of the Social-Emotional and Character Development Lab, and Co-Director of the Academy for Social-Emotional Learning in Schools at Rutgers University, USA. He also is a founding member of SEL4US, a national alliance of state social-emotional learning advocacy and implementation support organizations. Dr. Elias is the author of *Nurturing Students' Character: Everyday Teaching Activities for Social-Emotional Learning*, with Dr. Jeffrey S. Kress.

# Also Available from Routledge Eye On Education
(www.routledge.com/k-12)

**The Neural Teaching Guide:**
**Authentic Strategies from Brain-Based Classrooms**
Edited by Kieran O'Mahony

**Educators as First Responders:**
**A Teacher's Guide to Adolescent Development and Mental Health, Grades 6–12**
Deborah Offner

**Supporting Student Mental Health:**
**Essentials for Teachers**
Michael Hass and Amy Ardell

**Harnessing Formative Data for K-12 Teachers:**
**Real-time Classroom Strategies**
Stepan Mekhitarian

**Nurturing Students' Character:**
**Everyday Teaching Activities for Social-Emotional Learning**
Jeffrey S. Kress and Maurice J. Elias

**Differentiated Instruction Made Practical:**
**Engaging the Extremes through Classroom Routines**
Rhonda Bondie, Akane Zusho

# Reinvigorating Classroom Climate

## Everyday Strategies to Inspire Teachers and Students

Maurice J. Elias

Routledge
Taylor & Francis Group
NEW YORK AND LONDON

Designed cover image: Getty Images

First published 2026
by Routledge
605 Third Avenue, New York, NY 10158

and by Routledge
4 Park Square, Milton Park, Abingdon, Oxon, OX14 4RN

*Routledge is an imprint of the Taylor & Francis Group, an informa business*

© 2026 Maurice J. Elias

The right of Maurice J. Elias to be identified as author of this work has been asserted in accordance with sections 77 and 78 of the Copyright, Designs and Patents Act 1988.

All rights reserved. No part of this book may be reprinted or reproduced or utilised in any form or by any electronic, mechanical, or other means, now known or hereafter invented, including photocopying and recording, or in any information storage or retrieval system, without permission in writing from the publishers.

*Trademark notice*: Product or corporate names may be trademarks or registered trademarks, and are used only for identification and explanation without intent to infringe.

ISBN: 978-1-041-12143-5 (hbk)
ISBN: 978-1-041-12144-2 (pbk)
ISBN: 978-1-003-66320-1 (ebk)

DOI: 10.4324/9781003663201

Typeset in Palatino
by codeMantra

I dedicate this book to all educators, who work creatively, tirelessly, with love for their students, and a desire to see them succeed in school and life.

# Contents

*Acknowledgements*. . . . . . . . . . . . . . . . . . . . . . . . . . . . . . . . ix

1 Inspiring Students and Providing a Learning Climate in Which They Will Thrive . . . . . . . . . . . . . . . . . . 1

2 Educational Approach A: Creating Positive Classroom and School Culture and Climate . . . . . . . . . . . 17

3 Educational Approach B: Assessing Climate Informally to Ensure Its Quality . . . . . . . . . . . . . . . . . . . . 44

4 Educational Approach C: Encouraging Students' Strengths and Growth Mindset . . . . . . . . . . . . . . . . . . . . . 60

5 Educational Approach D: Promoting Sources of Inspiration and Human Dignity. . . . . . . . . . . . . . . . . . . . . 73

6 Educational Approach E: Articulating Personal Values and Sense of Positive Purpose . . . . . . . . . . . . . . . . 90

7 Educational Approach F: Cultivating an Attitude of Gratitude. . . . . . . . . . . . . . . . . . . . . . . . . . . . . . . . . . . 103

8 Educational Approach G: Developing Students' Intrinsic Motivation and Engagement . . . . . . . . . . . . . . 113

9 **Educational Approach H: Refreshing and
   Restoring the Soul of Educators**....................127

   **Conclusion**........................................135

   *Bibliography*.......................................137

# Acknowledgements

I extend my appreciation to my family, my wife Ellen, daughters Sara Elizabeth and Samara Alexandra, sons-in-law Josh Stopek and Paul Fisher, and grandchildren Harry Elijah and Isaac Ferris Stopek and Maia Jaye Fisher. Their love, support, nurturance, and understanding have allowed my work to continue through many positives and negatives in our lives. I also want to thank the many undergraduate and graduate students at Rutgers University with whom I have been honored to work and whose efforts would merit their own volume, and the many educators who have shared their work with me and accepted my work and ideas into their classrooms and schools. Finally, with great humility, I thank the editorial team at Edutopia, a project of the George Lucas Educational Foundation, which, for over two decades, has given me a platform to share blogs related to social-emotional and character development and related topics in education. This book is in large part the result of their generous permission to use these blogs in other writings. Onward!

# 1

# Inspiring Students and Providing a Learning Climate in Which They Will Thrive

Have you ever been in your car, listening to music on AM or FM radio, and you started losing the signal? For a bit, you probably heard two signals, competing for your attention. When this has happened to me, my typical reaction is to try a different station, or just turn off the radio altogether.

Believe it or not, this parallels what happens to students in school every day. Your outstanding lessons send a "signal" to the students. But their lives are often sending a different, conflicting signal. The two get mixed, with resulting confusion, discomfort, and frustration. Kids either "turn off" or they seek distraction elsewhere. Either way, they are not learning in a way that corresponds to your teaching. As this process proceeds for 180 school days, over multiple years, it's no surprise many students fall behind, give up, or leave school early.

No community is protected from these processes. Educators are in a competition for the minds and hearts of our students. We can't undo the difficulties and trauma students experience outside of schools. And we can't prevent those issues from coming into the school with our students. They can put their backpacks, books, and jackets in cubbies and lockers, but they can't leave their feelings behind in the same way.

As students go about their day, they encounter a lot that they did not know. This is supposed to happen! School is the place to learn what you don't know! But it can get frustrating. Students can feel "one down" and discouraged. Can you blame them? Would you like waking up, opening your window, taking a deep breath, and saying, "I can't wait to go to school for multiple remediation experiences today"?

Research and practice have taught us that there is a way to help our students learn more effectively, deal with their emotions more constructively, and tune into instruction more eagerly. It starts with the kind of climate we set up in our classrooms and schools. Are our students coming into places where they feel welcomed, cared for, and supported? Do our students know the core values that their classes and school stand for, such as kindness, responsibility, integrity, and the dignity of all human beings?

## Students Want to Matter and Have Positive Purpose

We also have learned that children and adolescents, like adults, want to feel as if they matter, as if they have importance and purpose. When kids are young, this can be accomplished by giving them opportunities to contribute to and help out during the class day. As they get older, these opportunities don't fade in value, but they need more. They need inspiration. They need to see what is possible for them to become, and to start to expand their aspirations accordingly. And this becomes the ultimate motivation to improve in academics. We need young people to say to themselves, "*The things I am learning will help me accomplish what I aspire to.*" Inspiration precedes remediation because children and teens will be more likely to engage in the hard and frustrating work of learning—especially what might come to them with difficulty—if they know that it will help them toward a valued outcome.

We need to expose students intentionally to sources of inspiration. To help ward off discouragement that might come from influences outside the school (including cultural biases), we need to actively build their sense of hope and positive purpose. In a society in which it is so easy to feel one can never attain what others have—even if much of what is portrayed on social media is far from realistic—we must build our students' sense of gratitude. Additionally, we need to bolster their intrinsic motivation, so that their aspirations and accomplishments are not under the control of external forces. "Some things matter because they matter to me"—that's the kind of self-talk we want to encourage.

To help in this process, I often use videos by Baruti Kafele that focus on youth purpose. "What is your purpose for walking into that classroom everyday?" is one of my favorites.[1] A video like this is one of many ways to get students to think explicitly about their purpose in life, what they want to live for, their positive aspirations, how they can make a constructive difference in the lives of others. It is from this mindset of "I matter, for good" that most students come to truly engage in learning. They have a reason to learn. Inspiration is a more powerful motive than remediation.

Of course, purposes young people identify in upper elementary, middle, or even high school are not likely to be those they retain throughout life. But evidence abounds that *having* a purpose (ideally a positive one) is a protective process against pessimism, despair, depression, anxiety, and surrender to negative peer culture. We know this from research and from accounts of how people are able to cope with extreme trauma, oppression, immigration challenges, and school disaffection by holding on to a sense of purpose. In a conversation between two individuals who span political perspectives, Ross Douthat and Senator Christopher Murphy, they were able to agree on this point:

It is true that this is a much less happy nation than at any time before in recorded data. We are a much more lonely nation and a much more disconnected nation. I think it's OK for leaders to talk about that and the fact that there are more people waking up every day who don't feel a sense of purpose like they may have 50 or 60 years ago.

Still, aspirations cannot be actualized unless our students have social-emotional competencies. They need to have the full set of skills that enable all of us to have success in the world… in our homes, workplaces, sports and performing venues, hobbies, civic life, and, of course, schools, including trade schools, colleges, and graduate schools. The competencies of social-emotional learning (SEL) are outlined in Table 1.1. This formulation draws on research catalyzed by the Collaborative for Academic, Social, and Emotional Learning (CASEL)[2] and are thereby typically referred as the "CASEL Five" skills.

You will see that there is more to being a social-emotionally competent individual than skills. There is attitude, purpose, and situational and cultural awareness and how and where these are directed, i.e., that they are positive, constructive, and prosocial. Arthur Schwartz, former CEO of Character.org, has said that character gives SEL its "why." This is consistent with recognizing that, as Theodore Roosevelt once noted, "To educate a person in mind and not in morals is to create a menace to society." For this reason, I refer to SEL as SECD: Social-Emotional and Character Development, or SEL 2.0. So, in this book, when I refer to SEL, you will know that I am thinking about this as SECD/SEL 2.0.

As you look at the skills in Table 1.1, try to find even one skill you would not mind your students lacking. I don't think you will be successful. The capacity to engage in all these skills is with most of us from birth. These capacities grow and mature through children's own developmental capacities and through experiences with various adults and peers and through interactions in various situations. Much of that development occurs in

**TABLE 1.1** Five Primary Social-Emotional Competencies (AKA "The CASEL Five")

| | |
|---|---|
| **Self-awareness** | • Identifying one's emotions, values, strengths, and limitations<br>• Having appropriate self-efficacy/growth mindset<br>• Feeling a sense of purpose, mission<br>• Taking appropriate risks/accepting challenges<br>• Trustworthiness and honesty<br>• Reflecting on one's actions, choices |
| **Self-management** | • Managing emotions and thoughts<br>• Establishing and achieving goals<br>• Persevering to overcome obstacles<br>• Focusing and organizing |
| **Social awareness** | • Identifying thoughts, feelings of others<br>• Taking varied perspectives<br>• Preventing and resolving conflict, nonviolently<br>• Showing understanding and empathy for others<br>• Knowing norms and expectations for different settings, situations, cultural contexts |
| **Relationship skills** | • Forming positive relationships<br>• Working in groups, teams—modulate, harmonize, lead, support<br>• Dealing effectively with conflict<br>• Using positive communication skills<br>• Knowing when and how to give, ask for help<br>• Constructively receiving and giving feedback<br>• Listening carefully and accurately<br>• Turn-taking |
| **Responsible decision making** | • Using effective problem-solving skills, strategies<br>• Identifying many aspects of consequences (e.g., long and short term, for self and others, direct and indirect)<br>• Evaluating the impact of one's decisions<br>• Analyzing and critiquing one's problem solving and decision making to learn for the future |

schools. Teachers' lives are made more difficult/easier depending on the social-emotional skills of their students. Building those skills depends a great deal on the climate and expectations you set up in the context in which you are working with youth. Helping you to do so effectively is the focus of this book.

In this book, you will read a series of short practice-oriented examples. Over a career of five decades, I have been blessed to visit and work with hundreds and hundreds of schools, in the United States and around the world. I have seen educators set up positive classroom and school climates, work with students to establish core values and respect for human dignity, inspire their students, foster hope, optimism, and positive purpose, build up students' sense of gratitude, and strengthen their intrinsic motivation. I have captured these practices in blogs I have written for Edutopia[3] over the past dozen or more years and present these here. In most cases, they have been edited to be as updated as possible; in a few instances, they are presented as they were published originally.

## Organization of the Book Around Eight Educational Approaches

This book is organized around eight educational approaches, roughly corresponding to what I have seen educators at their best carrying out, as I just described. At the beginning of each approach, there is a brief overview of the particular practice-oriented examples organized under that approach. This overview will help you see how the practice-oriented examples are related and support the effectiveness of the approach they represent. Of course, there are many more examples of how to carry out the approach than I have provided, and some examples certainly could fit under more than one approach. My focus in choosing examples is to emphasize what I have seen in practice and what is supported by evidence of effectiveness. If you are engaged in similar strategies represented by these eight approaches and they seem to be working, by all means, keep doing them. Add and adjust where you feel appropriate. A summary of the approaches and selected examples follows:

   A. *Creating Positive Classroom and School Culture and Climate*
   B. *Assessing Climate Informally to Ensure Its Quality*
     The first two sets of approaches address the climate of classrooms and schools. You can see a variety of ways to

bring a positive set of working relationships into classrooms and for students to feel as if they have something to contribute to their classroom, school, and wider world. Several informal approaches to assessing and improving the overall school climate also are included. Two elements of particular importance are educators being able to articulate the foundational role of culture and climate, and feeling a responsibility to help one's school organize a team that will take ongoing responsibility for monitoring and improving that culture and climate.

C. *Encouraging Students' Strengths and Growth Mindset*

The third approach, Encouraging Students' Strengths and Growth Mindset, is designed to help students identify and appreciate their own and other students' strengths and to see themselves as capable of accomplishments. By their nature, schools are places where children spend a lot of time not knowing. They often feel as if their days are filled with remediation and fixing. The practice-oriented examples in this section counteract those emotions and help students realize what they can contribute to the classroom, school, and wider world around them.

D. *Promoting Sources of Inspiration and Human Dignity*

Promoting Sources of Inspiration and Human Dignity contains sample lessons that help student explore who inspires them and to be inspired by individuals like Maya Angelou and Cesar Chavez and organizations like the Peace Corps. Students also become acquainted with the concept of human dignity and its role in diminishing contempt and hate in our classrooms, schools, and civic life. Students especially enjoy playing detective and solving the secrets of the Liberty Bell, exercising social-emotional skills to help them look more deeply at anything and everything they are learning.

E. *Articulating Personal Values and Sense of Positive Purpose*

The fifth approach guides students to begin to formulate answers to the questions: Who am I? What kind of positive person can I be? Why do I matter? Activities help students articulate their strongest values, identify and share possible purposes they might want to achieve in the future, and, most critically, see their schools as places that will help them reach their positive purposes.

F. *Cultivating an Attitude of Gratitude*

In our work, we have found that the next approach, Cultivating an Attitude of Gratitude, is of particular benefit when students are feeling "less than," underappreciated, or beset by trauma. Taking a "glass one-quarter full" approach has proven mental health benefits and redirects considerable vengeful and despairing energy toward learning.

G. *Developing Students' Intrinsic Motivation and Engagement*

All educators need to address the interrelated issues of intrinsic motivation and engagement. Especially as students go from elementary to middle to high school, they cannot expect to be reinforced for every good thing they do. This is neither feasible nor desirable. The seventh approach, Developing Students' Intrinsic Motivation and Engagement, provides brief but powerful tools to help students feel the profound, positive emotions that accompany intrinsic motivation. It turns out that activities that students find to be engaging also help build intrinsic motivation. Relatedly, students who are intrinsically motivated are easier to keep engaged in the learning process.

H. *Refreshing and Restoring the Soul of Educators*

The culminating approach is Refreshing and Restoring the Soul of Educators. Practice-oriented examples in this section draw from the work of Rachael Kessler, author of the *Soul of Education*, and Sargent Shriver, who made a speech entitled *The Hardest Job in America* (by which he meant teaching). Both recognize the irreplaceable role of educators in our society, the deep mission that educators carry with them, and their overriding concern to help students become better people who will make contributions to the world around them. Kessler and Shriver had profound appreciation for what teachers do—the practice-oriented examples show how and why teachers also should have profound appreciation for what they do.

In Table 1.2, there is a brief description of each practice-oriented example within each approach. All the ideas, suggestions, lesson plans, strategies, etc. that you will read have been successfully put into practice. Some of the examples are focused on early childhood settings, some in elementary schools, and some in middle and high schools. In many cases, educators have made adaptations of the suggestions to better fit the developmental levels and contexts of their students and schools. Regardless, through these suggestions, you can be igniters of your students' inspiration, sense of possibility and contribution, and positive social-emotional competence and character.

**TABLE 1.2** Eight Educational Approaches: Listing and Brief Summary of Practice-Oriented Examples for Each Approach

**A. Creating Positive Classroom and School Culture and Climate**

*Three Approaches to Building Positive Community in Any Classroom*
All students want to feel part of their classroom community. Here are three sets of activities to help them feel welcomed and comfortable.

*These Questions Help You and Students Learn More About One Another*
Discovering your students' answers to these questions can help you create positive conditions for learning.

*Have Students Create Their End-of-Year Legacy Now*
Here is an activity where students write their end-of-year legacy, revisiting it throughout the school year.

*Setting Up Schools and Classrooms to Be Engaging*
John Dewey's century-old words still hold true today and give us guidance on how an engaging school community is connected to learning.

*Creating a Positive Climate and Culture: The Role of Promoting Inclusiveness*
Learn about some classrooms and schools where social-emotional learning and inclusive curriculum go hand in hand for everyone's benefit.

*(Continued)*

**TABLE 1.2** (Continued)

*Improving Classroom Climate Reduces Bullying*
Improving the climate of classrooms for caring, respect, and learning cuts off the fuel of negativity in which bullying thrives.

*A Truly Socially Inclusive School Benefits Everyone*
Unified Champion Schools is a program of Special Olympics International that brings differently abled students together in various forms of shared activities and purposes for the benefit of the entire school community. Their ideas can work in your classroom and school.

*Chronically Absent Students Want a Welcoming School*
Getting students back in the building is just step one—next comes fostering a positive school climate so that they want to stay.

*You Need an Elevator Pitch About School Culture and Climate*
All educators must be able to articulate the importance of culture and climate as part of a process of assessing and improving it.

**B. Assessing Climate Informally to Ensure Its Quality**

*Evaluating Your School's Culture and Climate*
Creating a team to systematically evaluate how your school as a whole is doing can lead to valuable insights.

*A Feelings Walking Tour: Surveying Your School Culture and Climate*
Here is how to take a symbolic walk through your school to gain insight into the culture and climate and ideas for any necessary actions or changes.

*Social and Emotional Learning on the Walls*
The messages found on school and classroom walls should reflect the values that staff and administrators hold dear.

*What Kind of Ecosystem Is Your School?*
If we believe that a school is an ecosystem, then we realize we must care about every aspect of the school. Here is a humorous way to look at your ecosystem.

**C. Encouraging Students' Strengths and Growth Mindset**

*Guide Your Students Toward Positive Fulfillment*
Use these tips to improve your students' sense of joy, hope, awe, purpose, and deep connection.

*Finding Students' Hidden Strengths and Passions*
Here are some simple tactics teachers can use for uncovering students' talents.

*Student Goal Setting as a Path to Achieving Aspirations*
When middle and high school students set short- and long-term goals, they can see a path to the success they hope for.

*Building a Positive Mindset One Word at a Time*
Students can craft uplifting poems and narratives using a list of inspiring words you provide.

**D. Promoting Sources of Inspiration and Human Dignity**

*A Teaching Moment: The Peace Corps as a Source of Inspiration*
Reviewing the origins of the Peace Corps inspires some ideas for related service-learning activities.

*(Continued)*

**TABLE 1.2** (Continued)

*A Tool to Encourage Students to Respect the Dignity of Their Classmates*
The Dignity Index asks students to reflect on their thoughts about others and their willingness to listen to those with different views.

*Maya Angelou's Poetry: An Inspiring Lesson in Service, History, SEL, and Civics*
Maya Angelou overcame many challenges in her life to become a voice for peace and human dignity. This activity guides students to delve into her powerful poem "A Brave and Startling Truth."

*A Lesson About Cesar Chavez and Social Action*
As we wish to acquaint our students with inspiring leaders in democracy, social justice, civil rights, or nonviolence, Cesar Chavez is a person worth focusing on. Here is a lesson sequence that can be used in middle or high school to help students understand and be inspired by Cesar Chavez's activism.It may take a few classes to complete.

*Why Students Should Discover the Liberty Bell's True History*
Detective-like investigation of the history of the Liberty Bell inspires students to ask critical questions and look more deeply at the world.

**E. Articulating Personal Values and Sense of Positive Purpose**

*Helping Your Students Identify Their Values*
Have your students write about the principles they want to live by, using these prompts to help them get started.

*Guiding Students in Finding Their Truth*
What is your students' relationship with truth? It may seem like an odd question, but knowing your middle and high school students' relationship to the truth may tell you a lot about their character and their path to future success.

*Helping Students Find Purpose and Appreciation for School*
There are four areas that matter most to job satisfaction and productivity that teachers can apply to help students feel greater connection to their work in school.

*Developing a Sense of Purpose*
An essay prompt can help your students explore what drives them, showing them reasons to take on challenges in learning.

**F. Cultivating an Attitude of Gratitude**

*Habits of the Heart: Help Students Reflect and Act on Gratitude*
Here are several classroom activities to help students understand gratitude and put it to practice.

*SEL and Lessons in Forgiveness and Gratitude*
The Jewish Holiday of Yom Kippur yields lesson ideas for students on gratitude and forgiveness.

*Gratitude Builds Character and Health*
Expressing gratitude at our schools can build character and keep teachers healthy.

*Holidays or Holy Days: Strategies for Teaching About Celebrations*
Questions to use with students can inspire deeper thinking around December holidays and events, and appreciation for what we have.

(Continued)

**TABLE 1.2** (Continued)

### G. Developing Students' Intrinsic Motivation and Engagement

*How and Why Intrinsic Motivation Works*
Discover approaches for helping students feel personal autonomy, choice, and self-determination.

*Student Autonomy, Compliance, and Intrinsic Motivation*
The pressures of education today seem to be tilting the balance toward order and compliance, and this can have harmful long-term consequences for both children and society.

*Nurturing Intrinsic Motivation in Students*
Enabling students to experience accomplishments and improvement builds their feeling of competence—a powerful intrinsic motivator.

*"Do Now" Activities to Increase Student Engagement in Your Lessons*
Laura Weaver and Mark Wilding, authors of *The Five Dimensions of Engaged Teaching*,[4] have identified practical examples of how educators at all grade levels can add "Do Now" activities in their classrooms to help students stay engaged or become re-engaged.

### H. Refreshing and Restoring the Soul of Educators

*Restoring the Soul and Skill of Educators Through Engaged Teaching*
Remember why you went into the field of education: to educate the whole child—the curiosity, intellect, hearts, and souls of children—at all times.

*The Hardest Job in America*
This was the view of Sargent Shriver, founder of the Peace Corps, Head Start, Work Study, VISTA, Job Corps, and a champion for public school teachers. Reflect on his powerful words.

## Igniting and Inspiring Students' Learning

This book shares educators' primary concern: igniting our students' learning—social-emotional, academic, character, civic—and doing so via inspiration. This does not happen in a linear, programmatic way. Different students will be reached in different ways. The eight approaches presented in this book can be likened to an eight-piece quilt. To a novice, it may not matter which piece one begins with, which one is second, third, etc. At the end, the quilt will be completed; note that, despite using the same eight pieces, final quilts may look quite different.

However, there is one additional consideration: the impact of the quilt on the person. If we put a two-piece quilt on a child, he or she is not likely to feel warmth. Four pieces? Likely, something will be noticed. Whether there are six, seven, or eight pieces may make only a small difference in terms of warmth experienced. So it is with the eight approaches herein. They all make a difference, but as children experience four or more, they notice a change in their classroom, or school. And so will you.

That said, over the course of a career of nearly half a century, I have seen many quilts, and some ways of putting them together seem to lead to more warmth, faster, than others. Some pieces are foundational and hold the others together better. This is reflected in the order of the approaches in the book. The essential starting point for most students is for them to enter the school building for 180 days and feel a sense of safety, being welcomed, cared about, and listened to. It is the climate of the classrooms and school that opens great possibilities for students, especially their willingness to engage in self-exploration and sharing. Underlying this journey are the students' social-emotional competencies. What I have seen in schools now is that the climate is not one in which teachers are confident about formal teaching of SEL, and students are not especially receptive. They are most likely to tune out when they are recipients of multiyear approaches that are not well coordinated or engaging. So SEL needs to be added "in" and not "on top of" everything educators already are doing. Each entry is a gentle nudge to the reader, and something meant to fit into everyday routines and practices, i.e., added in, not on.

At the beginning of the examples from each approach, you will see an advanced organizer (Box 1.1). This is designed to help you shorten the distance between reading and putting the ideas you read into practice. In essence, I ask you to keep at the forefront the question, "How can I put this to use in my educational context?" That is the purpose for what I have written, and for what you are reading: to make an everyday difference in your work with students, their work with you and one another, and their relationship to what they are being taught. Take a few moments to look back on this chapter in light of the Reflection/ Application Guide, and consolidate your takeaways.

> **Box 1.1  Pedagogical Tool at the Start of Each Approach Section**
>
> The Reflection/Application Guide below is designed to help you bring the ideas in each of the practice-oriented examples into your professional practice. It is meant to serve as an advanced organizer. You may want to reproduce it to have available for note-taking as you read the various practice-oriented examples.
>
> As you are reading the practice-oriented examples linked to each approach, consider the following questions:
>
> 1. Visualize how a specific idea you are reading about might fit into your classroom/practice context.
> 2. Reflect on how this is similar to or different from your current practice.
> 3. Write three or four specific ideas you can most readily apply from the practice-oriented examples in this section.
> 4. Ask the author a question that might help to clarify, adapt, extend your understanding, etc. (SECDLab@gmail.com).

## One More Point Before You Read the Practice-Oriented Examples: The Evidence Base

There are few, if any, educational approaches with as much research behind them as social-emotional and character development (SECD). Two significant meta-analyses speak to the essential importance of SECD in educational and mental health outcomes. These and other sources are specified in the Bibliography. Recent research (see studies by Hatchimonji and Yuan in the Bibliography) also supports two fundamental premises of this book: that character and purpose add meaningfully to SEL (hence, the formulation of SECD by my colleagues and I) and that even the best social-emotional learning approaches must be built on a foundation of caring relationships and supportive classrooms and schools. But this is not news. I have been in the field of SEL/SECD for half a century, before this work was labeled as "SEL." It was clear from research back in the ancient times of the mid-late 20th century that caring relationships form the foundation of lasting learning. Any seasoned teacher could tell you that students' emotions affected their ability to take in even the best instruction.

Prior to the formation of CASEL, the William T. Grant Consortium on the School-Based Promotion of Social Competence, which I co-chaired along with the late Roger Weissberg, put forward the idea of "readiness" for skill acquisition. Importantly, though, this notion was not based on some condition in the child; it was based on properties of the classroom and school environment. Some of these properties, as has been said, were safety, concern, kindness, and support. In addition, children responded to a stance by the adults in the school that they were worthwhile, competent, had strengths, and could make contributions in the present and in the future. It is upon this foundation that learning—social, emotional, academic, artistic, civic—can be built.

However, especially in recent years to the time of this writing, and of no surprise to contemporary readers, educators have been under tremendous pressure to increase test scores. They have maximized time on academic tasks and have looked, understandably, for shortcut pathways to build students' essential SECD competencies. In doing so, they unwittingly have made success less likely by perpetuating the social and emotional obstacles making learning difficult for so many students. This book recognizes that educators need brief, practical solutions and that these first must be directed around establishing the conditions for learning. These solutions take the form of this book's practice-oriented examples, containing strategies that can be repeated throughout the school day and school year. They are designed to become part of the culture and climate of the school, how classrooms and schools go about the business of inspiring young people to learn. And once this is established, educators are ready to consider innovative ways of having SEL/SECD introduced into their academic instruction, not added on to it (which you hopefully will read about in my next book!).

## Notes

1 https://www.youtube.com/watch?v=U98d6CQbz4s
2 http://www.case.org/
3 http://www.edutopia.org/
4 http://www.solution-tree.com/five-dimensions-engaged-teaching.html

# 2

# Educational Approach A
# Creating Positive Classroom and School Culture and Climate

The Reflection/Application Guide below is designed to help you bring the ideas in each of the practice-oriented examples into your professional practice. It is meant to serve as an advanced organizer. You may want to reproduce it to have available for note-taking as you read the various practice-oriented examples.

As you are reading the practice-oriented examples linked to each approach, consider the following questions:

1. Visualize how a specific idea you are reading about might fit into your classroom/practice context.
2. Reflect on how this is similar to or different from your current practice.
3. Write three or four specific ideas you can most readily apply from the practice-oriented examples in this section.

> 4. Ask the author a question that might help to clarify, adapt, extend your understanding, etc. (SECDLab@gmail.com).

## Three Approaches to Building Positive Community in Any Classroom

Building positive community starts with the first day of school—actually, it starts beforehand. You can reach out to your students with a welcome letter to let them know how excited you are for them to be in your class and what appealing projects you plan to do over the coming year. This kind of communication has more positive impact than you might suspect!

Once they show up, students crave a sense of being a part of the community. Here are three groups of ideas to help them feel welcomed and comfortable. They are not one-shot deals. Rather, they benefit from frequent (i.e., almost daily) repetition, particularly during the first six weeks of school, and then regularly thereafter as ongoing reminders. I wish to especially thank my colleagues at the Northeast Foundation for Children who have thought and written about these matters extensively. Most of these ideas can be adapted to your age groups.

### Getting to Know You

In small groups, have students answer one to three questions from those below—or similar ones you create. Use a timer to give them 30–45 seconds to respond. Have groups share out one of the answers, or the most common answer. After the first round (which should have only one question to enable them to get started comfortably), help them learn how to keep track of time and to listen to what their classmates have said. Repeat other rounds over the next few days, or have students share the same things with different peers. Here are some sample questions:

- What kind of music do you like?
- If you could travel anyplace for free, where would you like to travel? Why?
- What is a place that you have visited that you like the most?
- When is your birthday?
- Where were you born?
- Who were you named after?
- Where do members of your family come from?
- What languages do they, and you, speak?
- What holidays do you enjoy, and how do you celebrate them?
- Have you ever been to a park, zoo, museum, or a farm? Pick one and tell us about it.
- What is a movie or a book you have seen or read lately that you really liked? Why?
- If you could be any animal that you wanted as a pet, what would you pick? Why?
- If you became the principal, what is one thing you would change about this school if you could?

## Take a Stand and Stand

Too often, students can be classmates, but feel disconnected from one another. Here is a way to help lower barriers. For each question, have all students stand if it is true for them. At any point, you can ask students who have areas in common to move to a spot in the room and share in more detail. You can do a few of these each day, especially to start a new year, marking period, or rotation of students through your secondary school classes.

Stand up if you:

- Were born inside/outside the United States (In the north? South? East? West?)

- Were born in this state/on an island (Someplace south of here? East of here? A map will help with this one!)
- Play an instrument (Percussion? Strings? Winds?)
- Play sports (With a large ball? Small ball? Soccer? No ball?)
- Like to read (Non-fiction? History? Fiction? Mysteries? Vampire stories? Sci-fi?)
- Know a quote from a book, poem, or lyrics from music (Who is the author or composer?)
- Like pizza (What kind? With mushrooms? Pepperoni? Olives? Onions? Extra cheese? Other toppings?)
- Like to eat dessert (Cold? Hot? Sweet? Creamy? With dough? With fruit? With chocolate? With peanut butter? Anyone with food allergies?)
- Can stand on one foot for five seconds (On the other foot? For ten seconds? Longer than that? Ask for demonstrations!)
- Like hot/cold weather (Being in the sun? Being in the rain? Thunderstorms? Windy days? Temperatures in the 90's? In the 20's? Anyone ever been in a tornado? Hurricane? Typhoon?)
- Know someone with a disability (Physical? Communication? Behavior? Cognitive? Other?)
- Have ever been part of a team (In school? Out of school? Music related? Sports related? Academic related? Other?)
- Have ever been to a concert/play/show/sports event indoors (Outdoors? At night? Did you sit near or far away?)

**Small Things Teachers Can Do Every Day**

All of these make more of a difference to students than we typically appreciate.

- Use students' names often.
- Establish shared agreements and rules with students.
- Enforce ground rules and agreements consistently with the help of students.

- Model behaviors of respect, caring, self-control, and fair decision making.
- Use energetic, enthusiastic, and receptive body language and words to convey interest and respect.
- Use a respectful *quiet down* signal to gain class attention.

## These Questions Help You and Students Learn More About One Another

Resilience and motivation come from having a sense of purpose, believing you have value to others, and engaging in acts of service that confirm that value. When these point in a positive direction, children gain momentum and positive accomplishment; when they don't, we see downward spirals and increasing distance from college, career, community, and life success.

There are some things we should know about all of our students because knowing them will greatly influence our teaching (as well as our parenting). They reflect the conditions necessary for students to learn, be happy, feel relevant, and be resilient.

Understanding who students are on a deep level also helps us be more understanding and supportive. In his article "Improving Teacher Empathy to Improve Student Behavior,"[1] psychologist and school-climate expert Robert Brooks explains that teachers increase their empathy by asking themselves, "What words do I want my students to use to describe me?"

The following questions can and should be adapted for youth of all ages because they are as relevant to college students as they are to preschoolers. Knowing the answers gives us insights into ways we can create positive conditions for learning.

### Questions to Ask Right Away

These start-of-school questions can be written out on index cards—ask children to write their answers on the other side, perhaps doing one per day during the first week of school.

- What helps you feel welcomed?
- How do you like to be greeted?
- What strengths do you bring to classrooms? The school?
- What do you like most about school so far? What would you like to see changed?

Another approach with these questions is to make a survey and have students provide responses; these can be anonymous or not. A more interactive approach is to use a morning meeting format and start the school day by having students discuss their responses to several of these questions in small groups and then share their group's responses with the class.

## Questions to Deepen Relationships

These settling-in questions can be addressed in similar ways as the start-of-school ones, during the second and third weeks of school.

- When do you feel competent? How often?
- When do you feel you are being listened to?
- When do you feel your voice is respected?
- When do you feel cared for and about?
- When do you get a chance to be a leader?
- When do you feel most safe/unsafe?
- When do you laugh at school?

## Questions to Use Throughout the Year

Use these questions throughout the school year, followed by supportive discussions, to continue to get to know your students, build their reflection skills, and positively influence their resiliency.

- What is your contribution to the school?
- Who believes you can succeed?
- What happens in school that makes you afraid? Frustrated? Defeated?
- When do you feel challenged and supported?

- What inspires you in school?
- Who helps you bounce back from setbacks?
- Who is always happy to speak with you?
- When do you feel it's OK to make a mistake, or show that you don't know something or how to do something?

## Growing Relationships and Trust

It often takes a few weeks before students get a clear sense of their answers to the initial questions. By then, they will know who believes they can succeed, and who is happy to speak to them and help them bounce back. (And during those first weeks, students will notice you hard at work becoming one of those reliable and trustworthy adults in their lives.)

The more we know about our students, the more we can help them find answers to these questions, which will allow their energies to be better directed toward building resilience and their growth as learners.

# Have Students Create Their End-of-Year Legacy Now

Here is an activity where students write their end-of year legacy, revisiting it throughout the school year.

Ask your students to imagine themselves at an assembly at the end of the school year. All of their classmates, teachers, staff, even parents are there. Every student is called up to the podium at the center of the stage, and the principal reads a statement of what they accomplished in the past year.

Here's a question for your students: What would you want the principal to say?

Inviting students to write their end-of-year legacy at the start of the school year is one of the most powerful and efficient social-emotional and character development (SECD) interventions you can do for students, grades 5–12. First, you get to teach them about the concepts of "legacy" and "reputation." You get to introduce them to the idea of being a person of character and deciding what kind of character they would like to have. Second, you start a conversation about character and accomplishment in the classroom, as students can share their legacy statements and then you can raise the question, "How can you support each other in accomplishing these important goals?"

Next, you can review the legacy statements at the end of each grading period, which can lead to a discussion, using these questions:

- How are you doing in working toward your legacy?
- What can help you make (more, better) progress in the next marking period?

You can repeat this process throughout the school year. You can integrate progress toward, and even selection of, the legacy into students' writing assignments. You can discuss the legacy of historical figures, as well as scientists, artists, poets, writers, people in current events, and ancestors.

Children who get into severe behavioral problems will be easier to support than they otherwise would be. You can help steer them back toward their legacies. It will also be helpful to discuss their legacies when students are sent to detention or suspension. Conversations with them can be directed with the question, "How can we help to get you back on track?"

Of course, at the end of the year, you may have to find a way to celebrate the accomplishment of many legacies, and help students think about how to continue developing their positive legacies in the following year. But at that point, the success you (and the students) will have experienced will make this extra work quite worthwhile. Establishing and working toward legacies is an SECD strategy that, aligned with researched-based best practices, can be a valuable part of your back-to-school plans.

## Setting Up Schools and Classrooms to Be Engaging

I have been reflecting on why, after so much education research, and so many years of educational practice, we still seem to be struggling to find "what works." So, I thought it would be valuable to look back at the words of folks who have thought about social-emotional aspects of school order and organization and created successful and effective efforts to promote them.

Here is what John Dewey wrote in 1915, over a century ago, in Chapter One of *The School and Society*. I have added italics to denote those parts of Dewey's message most relevant to school organization and engagement:

> A society is a number of people held together because they are working along common lines, in a common spirit, and with reference to common aims. The common needs and aims demand a growing interchange of thought and growing unity of sympathetic feeling. The radical reason that the present school cannot organize itself as a natural social unit is because just this element of common and productive activity is absent. *Upon the playground, in game and sport, social organization takes place spontaneously and inevitably. There is something to do, some activity to be carried on, requiring natural divisions of labor, selection of leaders and followers, mutual cooperation and emulation. In the schoolroom the motive and the cement of social organization are alike wanting.* Upon the ethical side, *the tragic weakness of the present school is that it endeavors to prepare future members of the social order in a medium in which the conditions of the social spirit are eminently wanting.*
>
> The difference that appears when occupations are made the articulating centers of school life is not easy to describe in words; it is a difference in motive, of spirit and atmosphere. As one enters a busy kitchen in which a

group of children are actively engaged in the preparation of food, the psychological difference, the change from more or less passive and inert recipiency and restraint to one of buoyant outgoing energy, is so obvious as fairly to strike one in the face. Indeed, to those whose image of the school is rigidly set the change is sure to give a shock. But the change in the social attitude is equally marked. *The mere absorption of facts and truths is so exclusively individual an affair that it tends very naturally to pass into selfishness. There is no obvious social motive for the acquirement of mere learning; there is no clear social gain in success thereat. Indeed, almost the only measure for success is a competitive one, in the bad sense of that term—a comparison of results in the recitation or in the examination to see which child has succeeded in getting ahead of others in storing up, in accumulating the maximum of information.* So thoroughly is this the prevalent atmosphere that for one child to help another in his task has become a school crime. *Where the school work consists in simply learning lessons, mutual assistance, instead of being the most natural form of cooperation and association, becomes a clandestine effort to relieve one's neighbor of his proper duties. Where active work is going on all this is changed. Helping others, instead of being a form of charity which impoverishes the recipient, is simply an aid in setting free the powers and furthering the impulse of the one helped. A spirit of free communication, of interchange of ideas, suggestions, results, both successes and failures of previous experiences, becomes the dominating note of the recitation.* So far as emulation enters in, it is in the comparison of individuals, not with regard to the quantity of information personally absorbed, but with reference to the quality of work done—the genuine community standard of value. In an informal but all the more pervasive way, the school life organizes itself on a social basis.

*Within this organization is found the principle of school discipline or order.* Of course, order is simply a thing which is relative to an end. *If you have the end in view of forty or fifty children learning certain set lessons, to be recited to a teacher, your discipline must be devoted to securing that result. But if the end in view is the development of a spirit of social cooperation and community life, discipline must grow out of and be relative to this.* There is little order of one sort where things are in process of construction; there is a certain disorder in any busy workshop; there is not silence; persons are not engaged in maintaining certain fixed physical postures; their arms are not folded; they are not holding their books thus and so. They are doing a variety of things, and there is the confusion, the bustle, that results from activity. But out of occupation, *out of doing things that are to produce results, and out of doing these in a social and cooperative way, there is born a discipline of its own kind and type. Our whole conception of school discipline changes when we get this point of view.* In critical moments we all realize that the only discipline that stands by us, the only training that becomes intuition, is that got through life itself. That we learn from experience, and from books or the sayings of others only as they are related to experience, are not mere phrases. But the school has been so set apart, so isolated from the ordinary conditions and motives of life, that the place where children are sent for discipline is the one place in the world where it is most difficult to get experience.

## Looking Forward

We are now rediscovering project-based learning, the importance of the school climate, why all students want and need a sense of purpose and accomplishment when they attend school, and how discipline problems are a byproduct of lack of engagement in school, and/or forcing students to be engaged in the uninteresting and non-involving. We see how character and social-emotional competence emerge not from instruction, or instruction alone, but from a classroom and school structure that calls forth values and behaviors of leadership, cooperation, mutual respect, consideration, self-control, teamwork, listening, and constructive problem solving and ethical decision making. A school that effectively prepares students for academic and life success has a democratic, inclusive spirit. Indeed, the spirit, or climate, of a school is greater than the sum of its parts.

These are principles we have known since 1915—actually, from well before that. But they have not yet become integrated into best practice, or standard practice. Sometimes we seem to be moving in the direction Dewey decries. It is up to all of us to know, stand up for, and do what is right for our students.

## Creating a Positive Climate and Culture: The Role of Promoting Inclusiveness

A commitment to being an inclusive school has profound effects on all students and staff. In each classroom and in all other school spaces, there is a shift in attitude toward empathy, support, and caring. Many more people in a school yearn for inclusion than those who might be legally or otherwise recognized as being someone for whom special inclusive efforts must be made. Here, I share with you examples of some specific ways that several New Jersey schools have used SEL-related approaches to foster best practices for classroom and school-wide inclusion and the creation of norms of acceptance and support.

1. Brigantine North Middle School, Brigantine, NJ: St. Baldrick's Day is a community and school-wide event and fundraiser for childhood cancer. Considerable preparations are undertaken leading up to the event, requiring use of many SEL skills. Activities include a lip synch contest, an eating contest, and a "baldminton" competition. Fire fighters and police join students and school staff in raising money to sponsor them having their heads shaved.

2. Thomas Sharp Elementary School, Collingswood, NJ: Climate survey data suggested students lacked Disabilities Awareness, and a program was created for that purpose. They kicked

off the program with an assembly. Embedded in regular class read-alouds, teachers included books about various disabilities. The author of *Keep Your Ear on the Ball* came to classes and discussed with students the impact of having a blind student in her classroom.

3. Memorial and Thomas Jefferson Middle Schools, Fair Lawn, NJ: Throughout the school year, students diagnosed with autism and Down's Syndrome are pen pals with students who are English language learners. Their correspondence builds language skills, awareness of cultural and other differences, and culminates in a meeting in May. General education and ELL students work together with special needs students across the district on science lab projects, written pen pal letters, and reading to one another.

4. Mendham Township Middle School, Mendham, NJ: Disabilities awareness is promoted by having each grade level read a specific novel focused on a child with so-called "visible" and "invisible" disabilities. Advisory classes reinforce the messages in the novels, providing time for students to reflect on the characters' strengths and difficulties and how they coped.

5. Livingston Park Elementary and Linwood Middle Schools, North Brunswick, NJ: Livingston Park has had in place an award-winning SEL program, Project Harmony, which exposes all students to peace education, conflict resolution, and prejudice reduction skills. A Family Circles program brings cross-sections of students and teachers together throughout the year on joint projects to create a better sense of belonging in the school. There is also a strong fifth-grade leadership program and Student Council that include students with disabilities. Mindfulness activities in classrooms help reduce tension and provide regular opportunities for stress relief. All fifth-graders participate in a disabilities-awareness program with Linwood staff and special education students involving experiences at five "stations": muscular mobile disability, visual process and learning disorders, dyslexia, blindness/visual impairment, and hearing impairment. For example, students must stack pennies

and color precisely with a sock on their hand. At the end of the program, fifth-graders get a bookmark with the slogan "Abilities Link Us Together" and share what they learned with their fifth-grade teachers.

**In Your Schools and Classrooms...**
These examples are inspiring and should prompt similar ideas that you can adapt. All the schools mentioned have learned that focusing on limited projects, such as a "day" or a "week" or two devoted to disabilities in some way, is not the answer: continuity is essential and that the cliché "slow and steady wins the race" truly applies here.

Bottom line: Many students would like to feel more included in their school. Any school can adapt the models illustrated here without disrupting (indeed, often enhancing) usual academic and school routines. Doing so will create a more positive, inviting, welcoming school climate.

## Improving Classroom Climate Reduces Bullying

Bullying takes many forms, including intimidation in classrooms by peers, or on rare occasions, by teachers. Intentional or not, when students don't feel safe to participate in the classroom, their learning is severely impaired. Even the most stellar curriculum cannot get through when students are worried about negative reactions when they participate in class.

Red Bank (NJ) Middle School, grades 4–8, took an evidence-based list of positive contributors to classroom climates (which you can find in Ed Dunkelblau's 2019 Laminated SECD Resource Guide)[2] and used it to create their own unique approach to improving the climate of their classrooms for caring, respect, and learning.

Here is what they did, adapted for your potential use:

## Creating Relationship-Centered Classrooms and Schools

What follows is a condensed list of classroom practices that create an engaging, supportive, caring climate for students (and staff). These practices also help improve students' social-emotional and character development (SECD). The first step is for teachers to systematically implement some of the items from the list below. In preparation for follow-up and discussion at a Grade Level meeting, each grade level team will collaboratively decide which three focus areas they will phase in and reinforce based on the timeline provided below.

*Timeline of Implementation*
- **Focus area #1:** implementation across grade level/content area from [insert date].
- **Focus areas #1 and 2:** implementation across grade level/content area from [insert date].
- **Focus areas #1, 2, and 3:** implementation across grade level/content area from [insert date].

Please place #1, 2, and 3 on the line provided for you below to designate your three focal areas:

- __Make sure bulletin boards and displays reflect the rich diversity of our students.
- __Model SECD behaviors of respect, caring, self-control, and fair decision making.
- __Pay attention to student reactions, need for clarification, and need for change in activity, and address the needs promptly, even if they must be addressed fully later.
- __Use "What do you think?" rather than "Why?" questions to stimulate divergent thinking.
- __Present and connect new skills and information to the students' responses and interests.

- ♦ __Respond respectfully to a wide variety of student responses to show respect and openness to divergent thinking, e.g., "Okay," "All right," "Thank you."
- ♦ __Share personal experiences from time to time to model and encourage appropriate and authentic student disclosure.
- ♦ __Take time at the conclusion of group work to discuss and debrief the activity so students can identify successful experiences and partner skills, as well as, set goals for improving group work in the future.
- ♦ __Emphasize positive roleplay examples and very clearly label examples of negative modeling.
- ♦ __Encourage students to discuss solutions rather than blame others.
- ♦ __Share my reactions to inappropriate behaviors and explain why the behaviors are unacceptable.
- ♦ __Make arrangements to meet with students outside of instructional time who continue to disregard the group/class rules.
- ♦ __Value social and emotional development as much as the cognitive development of students through the integration of SECD activities into the curriculum.
- ♦ __Create a safe, caring, and responsive environment, help all students understand what it means to be responsible, involved citizens of the class and school by modeling and encouraging participation in school events and using service-learning activities.

Red Bank Middle School had each Grade Level Team, Special Area Team, and Bilingual/ESL Team identify three focus areas that they will implement in their classrooms in a specified time period (usually across two marking periods). Teachers were asked to work collaboratively during Common Planning Time and decide which focus areas to identify as #1, 2, and 3.

Before finalizing, each grade level, as a team, shared which focus areas they will be introducing to their students, so that there is continuity and consistency within each grade level and to aide in planning across grade levels over time. Their final decisions were shared with the school principal, who would check in on progress and help provide resources as needed. The principal also used this information to set the process in motion for the following year.

### How Might It Be Useful to You?

By using this gradual approach, along with conversations that emphasized the literature on the importance of a respectful, encouraging climate for reducing bullying and improving learning, Red Bank Middle School got all of their educational staff involved in creating more positive classroom climates. They credit this as working with other efforts in RBMS to significantly reduce bullying in their school because any action selected as a focal area will create better relationships and connections for students in their classrooms.

Most important is to note that this approach conveys much respect to the professionals involved, allowing them latitude to identify what is most important to them, to work together as a team to afford continuity for the students, to have a gradual schedule for implementation, and to clearly know the implementation supports available.

These actions do not completely eliminate bullying, as there are some students whose circumstances are such that it will require more individualized and powerful interventions to reach them. However, their failure to respond to the kinds of actions above will be an early warning sign of difficulty and should signal involvement of a school mental health professional, ideally before negative behavior has a chance to escalate.

## A Truly Socially Inclusive School Benefits Everyone

Can a school have a positive culture and climate when its special needs students are not strongly included in the mainstream of all of its activities? This is a question that is not posed often enough in the social-emotional and character development worlds, but it is asked constantly in the offices of Special Olympics International (SOI). Within SOI, the Unified Champion Schools (UCS) program is tasked with creating ways to bring differently abled students together in various forms of shared activities and purposes, focused on the mainstay of SOI, sports.

Here is an overview of UCS and three case studies from schools that are walking the walk:

### What Is the Unified Champion Schools Program?

UCS is Special Olympics' effort to create a constellation of programs for schools and communities, focused on sports, that respects the dignity of all youth and empowers them to act as agents of change for young people with intellectual disabilities. While students with intellectual disabilities are the focus and have long been the impetus for Special Olympics' efforts, in practice, it is the genuine and respectful inclusion of all individuals (regardless of their specific abilities or lack thereof) that is desired.

The term that UCS uses often is "youth activation," and this refers to the need for everyone to see themselves as leaders and advocates for their own and others' well-being. Among the strategies used by UCS are:

1. UNIFIED Sports involving youth with and without special needs developing skills and playing sports together both during school time (often as UNIFIED PE) and after school.
2. R-Word Campaigns involving youth getting together to create videos, assemblies, and other school-wide and community programs to eliminate the use of the word "retarded."
3. Service-Learning and Leadership-Development opportunities including inclusive Student Councils, Best Buddies,

Youth Activation Councils, and Partners Clubs for joint service project activities.
4. Young Athletes focuses on toddlers and preschoolers and encouraging their motor development as a gateway to later sports participation.
5. Youth Summits and Forums where youth of varying abilities come together to share ideas, explore common social issues and community concerns, and generally enhance one another's common energy and capabilities.
6. Camp Shriver, a summer sports camp for inclusive skill development and competition.
7. Community Awareness and Education, which can happen through service projects as well as sport-linked activities like Fans in the Stands and UNIFIED Sports Pep Rallies and school or community-linked inclusive games and tournaments.
8. Volunteers, who have always been the hallmark of SOI, are involved in coaching, skill development, organizing events, fundraising, and numerous other ways of supporting inclusive activity.

SECD is at the core of how these programs work and succeed. It denotes the skills and attitudes needed for all these activities to come to fruition and to continue past the "event" stage, to become integrated into the school and community culture and climate. So, there is a strong and essential partnership between UCS's efforts to promote social inclusion and efforts that schools undertake to promote social-emotional learning and service, civic, and character education. Without social inclusion, can a school ultimately claim to be a school of character?

**Social Inclusion as a Superordinate Value**
All of the strategies and programs are designed to promote schools and communities in which the full and mutual inclusion of individuals with a range of abilities becomes the natural state. Social inclusion is viewed as a right, benefit, and value, not

only for those who might have the kinds of labels traditionally provided by our special education systems, but for everyone. Those who have participated in UCS and Special Olympics, more generally, can argue convincingly that those who have "done the including" have benefited from these events at least as much as those who have "been included."

The UCS program has extraordinary scope. It involves more than 10,000 schools across 50 states and has a growing international presence, as well. Nearly 1,700,000 young people have been touched by UCS projects and activities.

The UCS team is always visiting member schools, conducting interviews, focus groups, document reviews, and in other ways determining from all levels of the school and community what strategies were most effective in promoting genuine and deep social inclusion. They use evaluation information to improve program activities, especially toward longer-term sustainability. Here are three case study examples from which you can draw ideas to improve your classroom and school.

*White Pine Elementary School, Boise, ID*
This school serves 468 students in grades PK–6. UCS started in PE as a buddy program focused on fitness and friendship. Such programs focus on students helping one another become more physically able while enjoying one another's company and building stronger relationships. This was extended to Reading Buddies and then Lunch Buddies.

*James C. Wright Middle School, Madison, WI*
James C. Wright Middle School serves 242 students in grades 6–8, 83 percent of whom are Title I eligible. UCS activities are focused around an after-school leadership club enacting community service projects, such as Hoops for Heart and support of a local food pantry. This is part of a larger effort that extends into the school, via inclusive advisory periods, and an emphasis

on a school culture and climate that is actively affirming and respectful.

*New Iberia Senior High School, New Iberia, LA*
New Iberia Senior High School serves 1,591 students in grades 9–12, and when UCS was first introduced, the school had above-average dropout and special education rates. UNIFIED Sports was embraced by the football teams and coaches, leading to UNIFIED Flag Football including members of the Varsity and JV team. This has led to UNIFIED PE, an increase in socially inclusive activities after school, and much more active encouragement of special needs students trying out for and participating in a range of school sports clubs and activities. An ultimate result was a transformation of the mission statement: "NIHS, together with families and the community, will create a superior educational experience for all students by offering a positive and innovative learning environment."

What can you do to increase the extent to which all students (and staff, and visitors) feel as if they are welcomed and included in your classrooms and school?

## Chronically Absent Students Want a Welcoming School

Chronic absenteeism—defined as students missing 10 percent or more of school days—is a target area for many school districts for improving student achievement. This makes sense: Students who are chronically absent are more likely to lack reading skills, have lower test scores, and receive exclusionary school discipline, and they are in higher jeopardy of not graduating. And it's a big problem: Chronic absenteeism currently affects one quarter of all students, according to most estimates.

Typically, schools try to identify who is chronically absent and determine if there are cohesive subgroups of children most affected (recent immigrants, households with single parents, or caregivers with economic or health challenges). Sometimes the conditions that lead to absenteeism have more to do with family circumstances than student motivation. This is valuable and important information for school staff to have when deciding necessary supports for an individual child.

But it's not enough to simply get a student back on track with school attendance. Teachers, faculty, and staff need to continue their work in making all students feel welcomed at school. Finding ways to get students back into the building is step one, while continuously finding ways to let them know that they have genuinely been missed and are valuable to the community is the second-order change we need. Empty seats may have economic ramifications for a school, but continually filling the hearts and minds and raising the spirits of our students can have major social, emotional, and educational benefits.

### What Are First Steps?

According to the National School Climate Center,[3] creating a positive climate is the basis for academic success, social-emotional and character development, and the prevention of harassment, intimidation, bullying, and other problem behaviors. And studies show[4] a relationship between school climate and attendance in general—though so far this knowledge has not been directly extended to discussions of chronic absenteeism. But when we think of chronic absenteeism, an essential part of the long-term solution most likely involves getting all students to feel engaged in school so that they will want to be present.

As schools attempt to identify and bring back individual students with frequent absences, it is essential that the affected students feel as if the school is their oasis, not their holding cell. Schools must have a culture and climate that embraces all students and families. Young people have exquisite fairness detectors and know when they have been treated more punitively than another child.

## Creating a Welcoming and Positive School Climate

The Social-Emotional Learning Alliance for New Jersey[5] has worked to identify and develop some of the key elements of a positive school climate.

- *Inspiring*: Schools should connect to students' aspirations and actively encourage them to reach for the stars. Students should be asked to set specific goals for the school year and for each subject or class period. Goal setting should be a school-wide practice.
- *Supportive*: Challenge must be accompanied by support; schools benefit from collective efficacy, where students are encouraged to help one another. In the CASEL SELect Social Decision Making/Problem Solving program,[6] for example, elementary students are encouraged to set individual, ongoing character improvement and study skills goals and to buddy up with classmates to help in this process—improvement is not seen as an individual task, and setbacks are seen as a normal part of learning and an opportunity for mutual problem solving.
- *Safe and Healthy*: A supportive culture needs to be developed throughout the school, and in every classroom. Ultimately, we are each other's keepers, and so students must be upstanders for all classmates. They need support in learning how best to respect themselves by attending to their own good physical and social-emotional health, as well as others'.
- *Respectful*: Respect for others is an important expectation in a school building, and its modeling is essential—student to student, student to adult, and adult to adult—including parents and caregivers. Schools must be

especially attuned to how intimidating and unfamiliar school can be for some family members, such as those who are recent immigrants or those families struggling economically.
- *Engaging*: Learning defined as "engaging" is active and problem-focused, and it leads learners to create meaningful products. Classroom communities should set and pursue goals for learning together, and so should adults in the building—this includes teacher groups, student support staff, security personnel and school resource officers, office staff, grounds and maintenance personnel, and school administrators. All school members should have ongoing goals for improving themselves and their contributions to their schools, and work together to overcome roadblocks they meet on the way.

Public education is about opening the doors to learning and citizenship for all. Meeting this sacred responsibility is possible when our schools work to have a positive school culture and climate. If we build this, kids will come. And when they can't, once we help them with family and related hurdles and they do come, they are more likely to stay.

## You Need an Elevator Pitch About School Culture and Climate

When I asked a principal recently about the climate of his school, he said that it was often very humid because of poor ventilation. In another school, the principal complained about drafts in the wintertime. Those incidents, and others, have convinced me that some school personnel still need to be informed about school culture and climate.

Consider this. It's back to school night, and parents gather to hear what is going to happen during the upcoming school year. During a Q and A period, one parent asks you, "How are you going to ensure that this classroom is a place our children look forward to attending, and where they are eager to learn?" How would you respond?

Or what about this? Imagine you are in the elevator and in walks your district superintendent. It's the elevator in the administration building, so you know it's going to be a slow ride (at least 30 to 60 seconds). The superintendent says to you, "I understand you are in a leadership position in your school's culture and climate committee. What exactly is the focus of your committee, what's your understanding of school climate and why it's important, and what are your plans?"

The elevator door closes, and it's your turn to speak. What are you going to say?

## Creating Your Elevator Pitch

In both cases, you need an elevator pitch. It's also known as an elevator speech, but colleague Joe Cervantes suggests that the use of "pitch" is brief, focused, and less intimidating. I agree. Everyone in a leadership role (as classroom leader or as part of the school leadership team), when asked, must be able to clearly articulate what he or she (and the team) believe and are doing to create a positive culture and climate. While I will focus on the school context, you can easily see how this applies to the classroom level as well.

Often, it takes a little while to get oneself—and one's team—to comfortably speak about the climate and culture of the school. But it is potentially embarrassing to be in a leadership role and not be able to articulate what is happening. Imagine forward to a time when you and your committee members will be speaking with the staff, administrators, and maybe parents or school board members.

Everyone should be articulate and professional about what they are doing. Even if this kind of speaking is not your favorite thing in the world to do, as a professional, you still want to be, and appear, competent.

So that's why you need an elevator pitch! That pitch should include a definition of what the key terms mean, why it's important, and what the research says. And you should be able to deliver the essence in 30 to 60 seconds. Here are some starters for your elevator pitches.

## What Is School Culture and Climate?

### School Culture
This is the sum total of the behaviors and interactions of all adults and children, their attitudes and norms, and the extent to which the school is safe, supportive, healthy, engaging, inspiring, and challenging for all. Culture is what we do in the school or, as my colleague Marvin Berkowitz says, "How we *be* in the school."

### School Climate
This is the collective perception of how well a school provides suitable conditions for learning; for positive social, emotional, and character development; for all staff to grow professionally; and for parents, families, and community resources to become engaged in the school.

### Why Is It Important?
A positive school culture and climate is no different than clean air and water. It is the basis for sustainable learning and preparation for the tasks and tests of life. Conversely, research shows that in a toxic school culture and climate, learning by all will not take place effectively, and what is learned may be perceived in a negative way. When a school is a positive place to be, people are happy to be there, do their best, and make their best better.

## After the Elevator Pitches
Once a leadership team has helped the school community understand the importance of culture and climate, they are ready to

ask deeper questions to guide positive progress. This can happen systematically, but it usually is best to begin conversationally. So, school committees concerned with morale, discipline, and climate should ask:

- What is it that we are doing to help students (and staff) feel that this is a positive school, a place they look forward to coming into every day?

And then, with the necessary courage, ask the question:

- What is it that we are doing that is discouraging for students (and staff), that creates a negative climate?

An honest analysis of each of these, and the balance of them, sets the stage for taking specific steps to improving the culture and the climate. Once specific areas of need are uncovered, there are ample resources to guide steps toward improvement. And remember: Students will be an essential resource in making progress. It's their school, too!

## Notes

1 http://www.drrobertbrooks.com/improving-teacher-empathy-improve-student-behavior/
2 https://nprinc.com/social-emotional-and-character-development-for-teachers-for-students-for-parents-2nd-edition/
3 https://www.schoolclimate.org/
4 https://doi.org/10.3102/0034654313483907
5 http://www.sel4nj.org/
6 https://casel.org/guideprogramssocial-decision-making-problem-solving-program/

# 3

# Educational Approach B
# Assessing Climate Informally to Ensure Its Quality

The Reflection/Application Guide below is designed to help you bring the ideas in each of the practice-oriented examples into your professional practice. It is meant to serve as an advanced organizer. You may want to reproduce it to have available for note-taking as you read the various practice-oriented examples.

As you are reading the practice-oriented examples linked to each approach, consider the following questions:

1. Visualize how a specific idea you are reading about might fit into your classroom/practice context.
2. Reflect on how this is similar to or different from your current practice.
3. Write three or four specific ideas you can most readily apply from the practice-oriented examples in this section.

4. Ask the author a question that might help to clarify, adapt, extend your understanding, etc. (SECDLab@gmail.com).

## Evaluating Your School's Culture and Climate

It's clear that schools are more convinced than ever that attending to school culture and climate (SCC), as well as students' social-emotional and character development (SECD), is essential for success in school and life—for both the children and the adults in schools.

Schools are equally beset by what Patricia Wright calls the "I Can't Do One More Thing" syndrome. Wright, a former superintendent of schools in New Jersey and author of the acclaimed book *Sustainable School Improvement: Fueling the Journey with Collective Efficacy and Systems Thinking*,[1] shared insights with me into the dilemma facing many schools about how to realistically move forward.

### Everyone Must Know the "Why"

The work of SCC and SECD is not technically difficult. It's within the competence of any licensed teacher or school mental health professional to learn how to implement best practices in these areas. However, they are not typically emphasized in educator preparation, and their importance is not sufficiently understood. Hence, Wright advocates that educational leaders must have meetings, conversations, and professional development around helping teachers own and appreciate the salience of SCC and SECD.

This is not unlike how reading is at the core of all other academic areas. Teachers must have a chance to both question and personally articulate the "why" of SCC and SECD in the success of whatever role they have in the school. From an action perspective, priority should be given to SCC; SECD cannot thrive in a school with a negative climate.

## Systematically Address School Culture and Climate

Every school needs a school climate team that will keep a focused eye on creating and sustaining a positive, supportive climate for all students and staff. The most effective climate teams are treated as school committees, with monthly meetings of 60–90 minutes that are counted as part of educators' time, or stipended. The typical team will have several teachers representing grade levels within the school, a school mental health professional, a "specials" teacher, and a school administrator either on the committee or serving as a liaison/supervisor.

Wright has identified what she calls "ten conversations"[2] that help these teams get organized and ready for the tasks ahead. Foremost among those tasks is to set up an ongoing process for assessing the climate of the school.

"I highly recommend starting with a school climate survey that can be administered to students, staff, and parents/guardians," says Wright. "The responses from all three groups allow the team to analyze how the elements of school climate are viewed from each stakeholder's perspective, providing valuable insight that can drive the development of school climate improvement goals."

Disaggregated data on detentions/suspensions, bullying, and attendance also can reveal important trends. (This means it's also a good idea for at least one member of the climate team to be comfortable working with data or statistics.)

Of course, the point of knowing the climate is to improve the climate. Taking the time needed is essential, even if it's clear that the school climate is problematic. Wright suggests four steps toward creating a positive climate that echo my own experience.

## Four Steps to Assess and Improve Your School's Climate

1. Take an inventory of what the school is doing now to address school climate. Realistically basing future actions on

what is in place avoids "intervention fatigue" that can make even helpful initiatives feel burdensome. This inventory should include social and emotional learning and character initiatives, assemblies, discipline-related procedures and programs, and school rules around transitions such as entering and leaving school and lunchtime procedures, as well as programs for milestone recognitions and activities designed to boost teacher morale and provide support.

2. Ask the following questions about each of what is identified:

- What need is it addressing?
- Who is responsible for carrying it out? Is there accountability? Is this voluntary, or is the work involved recognized in some way?
- What evidence do we have that it is effectively addressing the need?
- Should we keep, modify, or abandon it?
- How does it fit with other climate-related efforts, and how can we ensure that all the pieces fit together well?

3. Get input from staff on what is in place, as well as ideas for changes.

4. Recognize and provide appropriate compensation or credit for the work of the climate team and ensure that the team is reporting at all staff and school-wide meetings.

## Don't Forget About the Interactions Among Adults in the School

One of the most telling climate questions I have posed in schools is to ask students (anonymously), "How much do the adults in this school like being here?" Staff are often shocked to learn that students are quite aware of their feelings about the school and their colleagues. When the school climate is truly positive, staff like to be there, students perceive this, and we often see a virtuous cycle of student–staff interactions. Wright outlines key steps for creating a collegial atmosphere in schools:

- Ask each person, including every administrator, to write a list of the expectations they have of a professional colleague.
- Have small, heterogeneous groups work together to come up with group lists.
- Share and discuss these lists and create an agreed-upon list of expectations.

Of course, lists are not enough. There must be explicit agreement to a final expectation: We will hold each other accountable for meeting these expectations in a spirit of mutual kindness and continuous improvement.

It's good to remember that the technical issues of improving the school climate are much more approachable once the "why" is broadly understood by all of the adults in the school, and by the students as well. Should climate progress revert, it's best to revisit the "why" before trying new programs. Once schools have embarked on the journey toward a positive climate, bringing in ways to improve social-emotional and character development is considered wind in the sails, rather than a hindrance.

## A Feelings Walking Tour: Surveying Your School Culture and Climate

Take a walk through your building or workplace and attend to the feelings you have. No, not an actual walk—a symbolic one. By so doing, you will learn a lot about the culture and climate of your school and some areas where action may be needed.

Close your eyes and picture yourself arriving at school, walking in, and moving from place to place over the course of a typical day. Pay attention to the entrance ways, what you see on the walls, the furniture and how it's arranged, and the main office. How welcoming is it?

Look in on classes, lunch and recess times, hallways and staircases, trailers and far-off wings of the building, meetings, extracurricular activities, after-school, and evening events—the entire gamut of what occurs on regular school days. Finally, imagine yourself preparing to leave, visualize your departure process, and then open your eyes.

Now ask yourself some questions about what you experienced:

- Where and when do you experience "positive" emotions such as pride, joy, and excitement?
- Where and when do you experience "negative" emotions such as anxiety, frustration, and anger? Where do you experience both types of emotions?
- Where do you detect harassment, intimidation, and/or bullying going on?
- Where do you see the most student peer-to-peer, adult-to-student, and adult-to adult support?
- What is happening in these places to cause these emotions?

Based on an activity from *Building Learning Communities with Character: How to Integrate Academic, Social, and Emotional Learning*,[3] this process can be done individually or with a team—grade level, department, or entire faculty—and can give you great insight about your school as a learning environment. It will tell you about places that need to be changed, as well as those whose good qualities need to be preserved and expanded. Of course, it's hard to be objective about your own setting within the school. You may want to ask some of your colleagues to take a scaled-down "walk" past *your* location and report their feelings and reactions to you.

What comes next? We know the path from insight to action is neither obvious nor easy. So, there are a couple of questions to ask yourself: What feelings are most likely to serve as catalysts for action in your setting and who are your allies in taking systematic and sustained action?

## Social and Emotional Learning on the Walls

I once worked with a colleague who focused on social and emotional learning (SEL) for parents. She always maintained that anything that is important to a family is either on the refrigerator or in it. She made a point of designing materials that could be put on the fridge with magnets that would remind parents of ways to prompt SEL in their kids on a daily basis.

I was reminded of this in October 2024, when a delegation from the Singapore Ministry of Education visited schools in Paramus, Montville, and Roselle, New Jersey, to see how these buildings put SEL into action. These schools have powerful, optimistic visions of their students' futures and see SEL as essential to student success in school and life. Some of their schools have received Promising Practices and School of Character awards from Character.org[4] and have been recognized by New Jersey's School Culture and Climate Initiative.

### "A CT Scan of the Soul"

I couldn't help but notice the attention that the delegation paid to the walls of the classroom and the hallways of the school. I was curious about this and was informed that regardless of what people might tell you they are doing, what they have created and placed on their walls is a great clue to what they value the most. One person described it as being like "a CT scan of the soul."

The delegation was looking at the walls for answers to certain questions—questions that almost always were answered with some version of "yes."

Here are examples from the three New Jersey school districts we visited and some others.

## Emphasizing SEL Skills and Core Values

The most powerful indicators of core values are not signs that state them, but rather work displayed that integrates them and puts them into action. In one school, every day, in addition to saying the Pledge of Allegiance, middle school students recite these pledges that they co-created and posted on classroom walls, embodying the school's core values:

> *Pledge to Myself*
> *This day has been given to me fresh and clean.*
> *I can either use it or throw it away.*
> *I promise myself I shall use this day to its fullest, realizing it can never come back again.*
> *I realize this is my life to use or throw away.*
> *I MAKE MYSELF WHAT I AM.*
>
> *Pledge to the Universe*
> *I pledge allegiance to the world*
> *To cherish every living thing*
> *To care for EARTH, SEA, and AIR*
> *With PEACE and FREEDOM everywhere!*

## Applying SEL Skills to Academics

One way of applying skills to academics is to ask students to write letters to characters in books they are reading that reflect the SEL or character lessons they are receiving. One of my favorites was posted on a bulletin board in a first-grade classroom where students participated in the Rutgers University Social Decision Making/Problem Solving Program (SDM/SPS):[5]

> Dear Big Bad Wolf,
> You shouldn't kill the little pigs! Let them live. You need SPS. You've got problems!
> From, Wally

In other classrooms, during social studies, students were asked to write or draw responses to the questions, "What do I think would make the world a more peaceful place?" and "What are ways to be more conscious of our classroom and school environment?"

### Applying SEL Skills to School Issues

Almost all SEL programs include a systematic problem-solving strategy that students learn. Have students use this strategy and/or core values to propose solutions to school problems that are then posted on the walls as reminders about how to handle certain situations.

In one class, each student was asked to write about the theme of "No Violence" based on their school's problem-solving model and core values. Groups of responses were posted on the wall on a rotating basis. Here is one example:

> There should not be any violence in this school. Not even at any other school. We need to Stop, Choose, and Move On. We need to persevere and not fight. We have to respect other people's boundaries. No violence! Persevere! Be kind to others!
>
> Lila, second grade

### Reflecting Positive Commitment to the Classroom or School

The site visitors felt that messages from teachers to their students posted on the wall as a constant and tangible reminder of support can be inspiring to students and a good reminder to teachers about the bigger picture of their work. Figure 3.1 is a message from one fourth-grade teacher.

### Reminding Students About Key Strategies

Expecting students to remember everything they learn in SEL—or any—lessons is not a realistic strategy. By posting reminders of key strategies, teachers make it more likely that students will bring those strategies into everyday classroom interactions. The following was posted in a fourth-grade classroom.

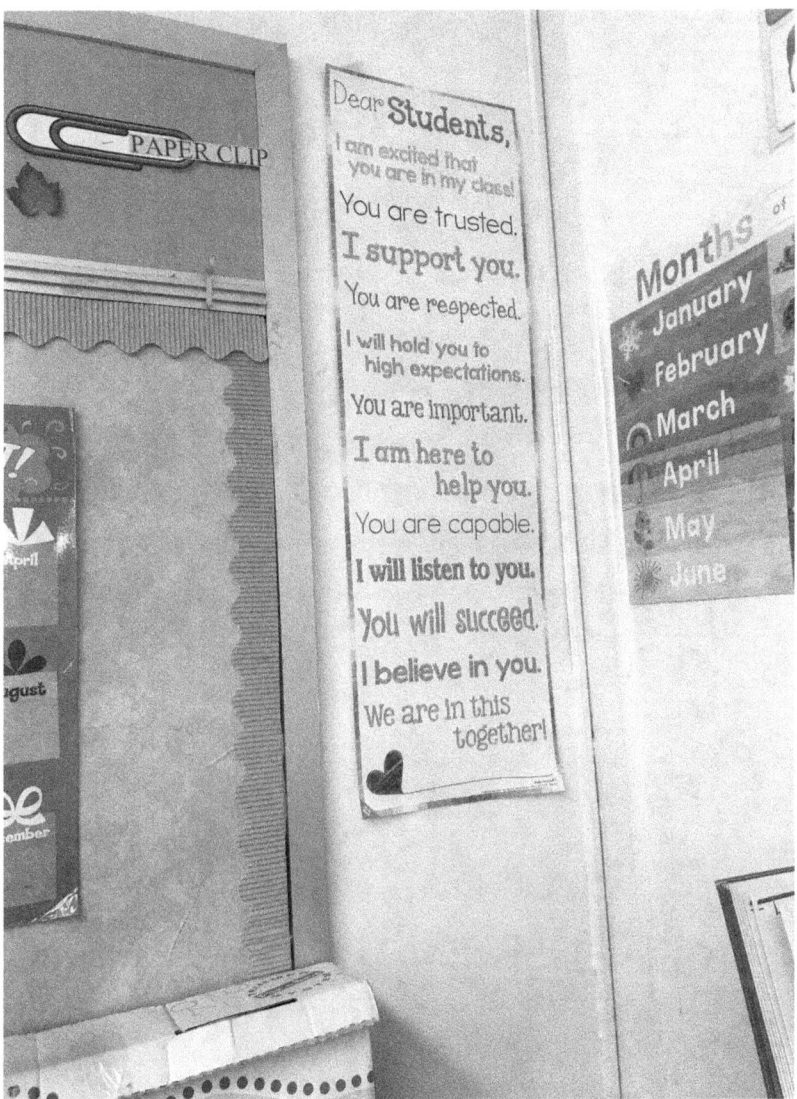

**FIGURE 3.1** An Affirmation of Students from Their Teacher

How to Solve Problems

1. What is the problem?
2. What are some solutions?
3. For each solution, ask:

   Is it safe?

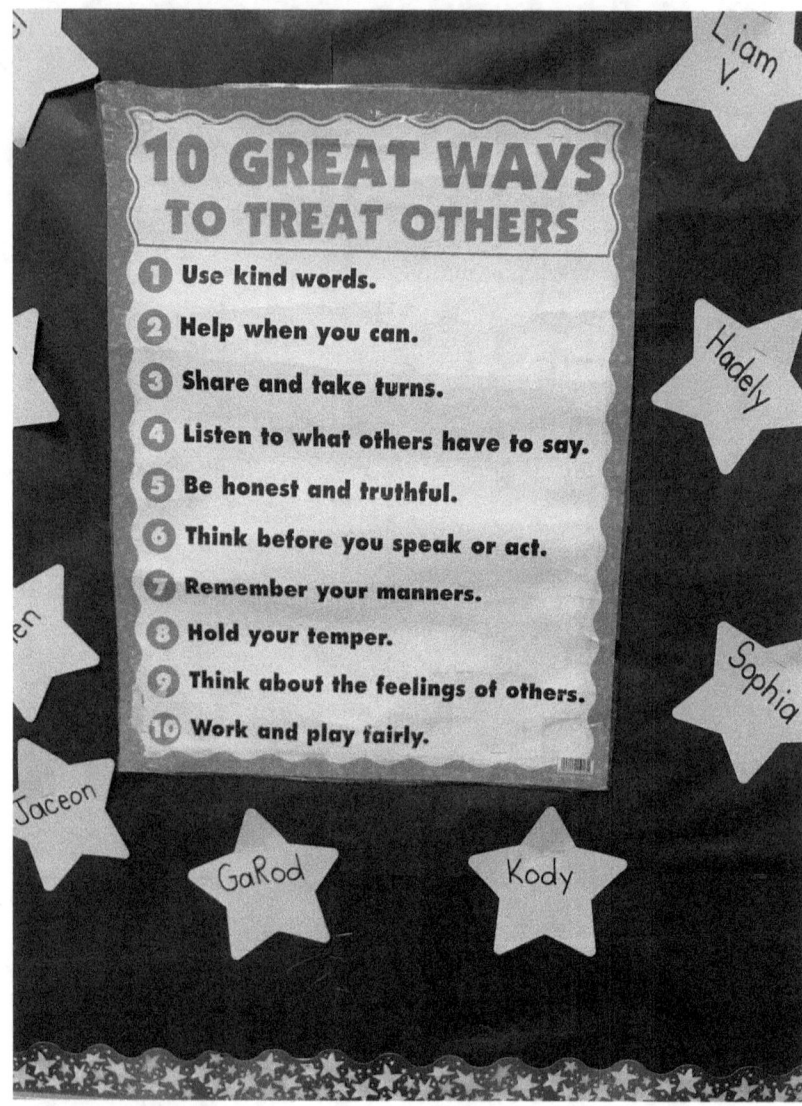

**FIGURE 3.2** 10 Great Ways to Treat Others

How might people feel?
Is it fair?
Will it work?

4. Is it working? If not, what can I do now?

### Reminders About Caring, Kindness, and Support

As with the SEL strategies, reminders about relationships improve the classroom climate and help students reflect on their own behavior. These are most effective when co-created with your students. The poster in Figure 3.2 was found in a second-grade classroom.

A combined fourth- and fifth-grade classroom displayed the following:

What Makes a Friend a Friend
F—Forgives you
R—Respects you
I—Involves you
E—Encourages you
N—Needs you
D—Deserves you
S—Supports you

As the delegation completed its visits to schools, Montville school counselor Doug Stech spoke to how engaging youth directly "activates SEL skills and fosters inclusiveness. We made a change from finding joy in success to finding success in joy." And Roselle superintendent of schools Dr. Nathan Fisher provided an apt summary: "There is no 'Roselle' without SEL." We might take the liberty of saying there is no SEL learning without the walls speaking.

## What Kind of Ecosystem Is Your School?

A school is an ecosystem. One dictionary definition of "ecosystem" is: "a biological community of interacting organisms and their physical environment." If we believe that a school is an ecosystem, it has tremendous implications for how we organize schools and conduct ourselves within them.

My thoughts about this were crystallized from a recent trip to Costa Rican rainforests and biological preserves. A fundamental principle of an ecosystem is interdependence. This means that something that happens in one part of the system affects other parts of the system.

Another fundamental principle of ecosystems is that they are designed to adapt and thrive. So, when alterations are made, say, due to policies like deforestation to gather wood for commercial uses or circumstances such as global warming, there can be severe negative consequences. The patterns of relationships of weather, soil, and access to food and other resources become disrupted. These can threaten certain species or lead them to change their behavior over time in unpredictable, often harmful, ways.

## Every Element in a School Affects Other Parts

If you have not yet drawn the analogy to our regimen of high-stakes testing, attempts to link teacher evaluations to salary, and otherwise scripting education to make it "teacher proof," you should do so.

Adam Grant, writing in the *New York Times* ("Week in Review," January 31, 2016), showed that regimens of practice designed to develop prodigies, and related "drill-repeat-test" routines that we see most often in remedial contexts, lead to counterproductive results. To quote one example: "Top concert pianists didn't have elite teachers from the time they could walk; their first lessons came from instructors who happened to live nearby and made learning fun".

If we believe that a school is an ecosystem, and act that way, then we shift our perspective. We realize that every element of a school affects other parts. How our least-advantaged and most at-risk students are treated affects the success of the entire school. How teachers treat each other and students matters. How lunch aides treat students and are treated by other school professionals also matters.

If we believe that a school is an ecosystem, then we realize that classrooms are ecosystems, also. We become more sensitive to the nuances of policies that we set into schools. We look at their effects in everyday, not only longer-term, ways. We redefine *high stakes* to not only refer to testing but also to include daily interactions, and the mind, heart, hands, and soul of all those touched by our policies. Small things matter.

If we believe that a school is an ecosystem, then we realize we must care about every aspect of the school. The school itself is the product of all of the interactions and interdependencies of all of its components, regardless of visibility. And a school district is an even wider ecosystem, and one that is defined by how it embraces its most troubled schools as much as how it treats its best. Indeed, just as corporate inequities are built on the backs of the least cared-for workers, educational inequities are built on the backs of the least cared-for students and staff.

Walking through the rainforest, and other ecosystems in Costa Rica, I realized that the wisdom to know what parts of the ecosystem possess less importance than others is beyond us. Drawing this analogy into schools, we have an ethical and moral obligation to nourish the ecosystem of the school by supporting all of its parts, to allow every student to develop his or her capacity to thrive in ways that will make a positive contribution to the whole.

### How Many Turtles? How Many Raccoons?

Please read the descriptions of each of the rainforest residents below, and determine who, in your school—or team, group, or committee—is a representative of that resident. (Thanks to my travel companions in Costa Rica for their input on this!) The tracking system is itself ecological; you can figure out whether you have too many of some and not enough of others:

**Macaw:** The macaw is renowned for its loyalty. Though not averse to straying on occasion, it always comes back to its senses.

**Crocodile:** The crocodile is ancient, formidable, and has a powerful jaw quick to snap shut with many sharp teeth. It adapts well to all kinds of circumstances and is not to be messed with.

**Turtle:** Though a symbol of deliberate wisdom, turtles are pretty ornery and retreat into their shells in response to threat. They stick to highly routinized patterns and are resistant to changes, but have seen quite a bit.

**Howler Monkey:** The howler monkey is incredibly loud and can be heard from miles away. It uses its howl to disconcert and threaten, but it retreats when confronted.

**Three-toed Sloth:** The three-toed sloth is very slow moving and not concerned much about others around it. It saves negative things up for a week and then spews them out, though not with an intent to harm—but it still harms those in the way.

**Capuchin Monkey:** The capuchin money is very social and involved in everyone's business. It operates in cliques and is not hesitant to take what belongs to others.

**Frog:** Frogs are highly nurturing, especially of newbies. They are willing to put aside their own well-being to help the next generation emerge in a healthy way.

**Manuel Antonio Park Raccoon:** These raccoons are focused on extrinsic motivation; they act when they think they can benefit, and so are open to being led by and oriented toward tangible rewards—even to their own detriment.

**Spider Monkey:** The spider monkey swings from tree to tree with little focus. It likes to show off and be seen.

**Bat:** Bats are an essential part of the rainforest and are highly varied. Some help pollinate, bringing seeds to different parts of the rainforest; some attack small, defenseless animals, and even infants; and some help control the mosquito population, minimizing those annoying ecosystem residents.

### Look at Your Classroom

It's fun to look at a classroom and see how students' personalities may correspond to the denizens of the rainforest. You may find yourself needing to invoke other animals or considering combinations. Some students may need to be a little more capuchin monkey, others, less Manuel Antonio Park raccoon.

### School Turnaround Means Improving School Climate

Schools cannot be "turned around" without treating them like ecosystems. Schools cannot produce proficiency, let alone excellence, without attending to the climate of the school and the social-emotional competence and character of everyone in the school.

This calls into question the usual way a lot happens in education. Our policies and programs tend to be fragmented, not holistic. Too often, they focus on subject areas and content, rather than on the people in the schools and their relationships to one another and to the material being taught. When you want to start down the road of school improvement or turnaround, it's time to gather your macaws, turtles, frogs, maybe even a crocodile or two, and set a direction that will eventually draw in everyone in the ecosystem.

## Notes

1 https://www.bloomsbury.com/us/sustainable-school-improvement-9781475862867/
2 https://wpvip.edutopia.org/wp-content/uploads/2023/08/Ten_School_Climate_Team_Conversations.pdf
3 http://www.ascd.org/Publications/Books/Overview/Building-Learning-Communities-with-Character.aspx
4 https://character.org/what-we-stand-for/
5 https://socialdecisionmaking.com

# 4

# Educational Approach C
# Encouraging Students' Strengths and Growth Mindset

The Reflection/Application Guide below is designed to help you bring the ideas in each of the practice-oriented examples into your professional practice. It is meant to serve as an advanced organizer. You may want to reproduce it to have available for note-taking as you read the various practice-oriented examples.

As you are reading the practice-oriented examples linked to each approach, consider the following questions:

1. Visualize how a specific idea you are reading about might fit into your classroom/practice context.
2. Reflect on how this is similar to or different from your current practice.
3. Write three or four specific ideas you can most readily apply from the practice-oriented examples in this section.

4. Ask the author a question that might help to clarify, adapt, extend your understanding, etc. (SECDLab@gmail.com).

## Guide Your Students Toward Positive Fulfillment

> We must remember that intelligence is not enough. Intelligence plus character—that is the goal of true education.
>
> Dr. Martin Luther King, Jr.

Have you thought about ways to help cultivate the character of your middle and high school students? If you consider social and emotional learning skills as the engine that enables accomplishment, you might want to look at character as the steering wheel that gives young people a sense of direction. Might character be as worthy of our attention as academics, civic competencies, and artistic literacy—and perhaps be connected to all three?

I heard Eliot Malomet, a rabbi in New Jersey, pose a compelling analogy. He said that when we go for a medical exam, our vital signs are typically assessed through measures of body temperature, pulse, respiration, blood pressure, and blood oxygen levels. Thinking about how our society is marked with so much activity, but lacking in depth and focus, Malomet speculated on a measurement of people's sense of fulfillment, identifying five vital signs: contentment/joy, hope, awe, meaning/purpose, and deep connection.

### Five Signs of Fulfillment

I believe these five vital signs can help us guide youths toward positive fulfillment. I have put them in the form of questions that you can present to your students (and to yourself). I've also included scales you might use as informal metrics and as guidance for improving each area:

### 1. Contentment and Joy

How much do you experience both joy and satisfaction in your life? *(5) almost constant; (4) most of the time; (3) half of the time; (2) some of the time; (1) almost never*

Guidance: This is deceptively simple. Many people agree that we are content when our lives are going reasonably well and when we are being of service to others[1]—family, classmates, colleagues, the community, and even strangers. But we also need some joy in our lives—moments that light us up and bring us smiles. This kind of joy[2] comes from celebrating positive events with people we cherish.

### 2. Hope

To what extent do you look ahead in your life with optimism, positive expectation, and anticipation of accomplishment? *(5) almost always; (4) most of the time; (3) half of the time; (2) some of the time; (1) almost never*

Guidance: When youths are pessimistic, see little chance of reaching positive goals, and feel hopeless, we cannot expect to see their best efforts at learning or good behavior. We must work with their strengths and teach them to set and reach small goals so they can build a hopeful sense of accomplishment.

### 3. Awe

How often do you experience a sense of wonder, amazement, and astonishment? *(5) several times recently; (4) once recently; (3) once in the past month; (2) once in the past year; (1) almost never*

Guidance: We need to lift our students' horizons by helping them appreciate the wonder around them: the miracle of a rainbow, a sunrise, how our bodies function, and the amazing ingenuity and goodness some people display. Even when life is difficult, a sense of awe helps us keep going.

And there is a lot to hold in awe, once we start to focus on it. Doing so can shift our perspective in ways that allow our thoughts and feelings to soar. Experiencing awe and wonder must be more than an annual event for our youths (and for adults).

*4. Meaning/Purpose in Life*
Can you point to things in your life that give you positive meaning and purpose? *(5) definitely yes, more than one; (4) maybe one thing; (3) not sure; (2) only in the past; (1) never*

Guidance: I call out *positive* because research tells us[3] that when some youths are not able to see pathways to prosocial purposes, they shift to antisocial ones. Having a sense of purpose and meaning is linked with fulfillment and is a normal sign of health. Because its absence is unsettling to individuals, it is not surprising to see youths and older people choose a negative purpose over no purpose. Consider why some children actively seek the role of class clown or bully.

*5. Deep Connection*
When do you have a sense that you are connected to something, or someone, bigger than yourself? *(5) all the time; (4) most of the time; (3) some of the time; (2) a little of the time; (1) never*

Guidance: Rachael Kessler made it clear in The Soul of Education[4] that connecting to something greater than oneself is a desirable part of development, especially in adolescence. It fuels idealism, learning, adventure, leaving comfort zones, and other actions that give youths energy and seem to make them feel as if their capacity and potential are limitless. It also tides them over in times of difficulty.

## Cultivating a Sense of Fulfillment

All five of these areas—contentment/joy, hope, awe, meaning/purpose, and deep connection—are related to one another. Cultivating even one of these in our students can help advance the others when they are lacking. Our schools need to be places of inspiration where social and emotional learning and character development are engaged intentionally and as often as academics.

## Finding Students' Hidden Strengths and Passions

Brad Hirschfield is the President of the National Jewish Center for Learning and Leadership[5] and he has spent a lot of time thinking about how to foster both learning and leadership. He has some ideas about how we can inspire our students by helping them find their hidden strengths and passions.

To use the word "hidden" may not be quite accurate because often, strengths are hidden by lack of opportunity to display them. Too often, when students are in school, they are not looked at in terms of their strengths; rather, there is a focus on remediating their deficits. This is rarely a source of inspiration for anyone. What ends up happening is that young people's strengths and passions are either hidden from their educators or worse, they become hidden from the children themselves because they do not get encouraged.

So, what can educators do? First, have all your students tell you about their hobbies or other things they really like to do or are very good at. You can do that in a homeroom or advisory, or you can work it into a language arts or other assignment. There is a benefit to having everyone go around and share with classmates. Typically, their classmates also are unaware of their assets.

Second, ask students to talk about times when they found out something surprising and good about someone else. Ideally, this would make a wonderful topic for an essay or short story or even an art-related assignment. From these examples, help students reflect on things about themselves that classmates or teachers might find surprising or impressive.

Third, have students talk to their parents or guardians about their "hidden talents"—you may want to use this exact term. Help them develop a short interview schedule to find out about hobbies or aspirations that family members may have pursued at one time and then had to give up, or decided not to follow up. Consider making a scrapbook for presentation to parents (this can be a digital scrapbook for easy sharing), something that they might even find a bit inspiring.

You may have your own ideas. Colleagues in Israel use a program developed by Josef Levi when he was Superintendent of the Tel Aviv Central School District, Israel's largest. Dr. Levi would reserve Friday afternoons for all students in multi-grade groupings to do projects based on their multiple intelligence strengths. These projects ranged from students who wanted to make some kind of aircraft, to students making robots, creating artwork, doing a chess-related project, creating a fashion show, and songwriting and performing. Each had an academic component linked to the curriculum and each one had a powerful motivating effect on many of the students.

Brad Hirschfield reminds us that miraculous discoveries must be actively uncovered. That is, action must be taken to find what is hidden. Let's be sure we are taking those actions so that our students do not lose some of their most deeply treasured possessions—their strengths and passions—and instead see their classrooms and schools as places where these are valued.

## Student Goal Setting as a Path to Achieving Aspirations

> If we did all the things we are capable of, we would literally astound ourselves.
> Thomas Edison

I learned that quote from Wendy Beth Rosen's *Self-Smart*. Taking it seriously, Wendy suggests some areas where students'—and adults'—self-assessments can lead to greater accomplishments and personal satisfaction. Many distractions and challenges in our lives threaten to throw us off our path or keep us from knowing what our path is. Setting explicit goals for what we most want to accomplish and tracking our progress toward them is a way to increase our chances of finding the success we hope for.

Here is a method of goal-tracking that can be used by students and educators in ongoing ways, as well as at specific points when experiencing uncertainty or setbacks. These also have value for promoting positive mental health in schools.

## Setting and Tracking Goals

Middle and high school are particularly important times for students to become consciously aware of and intentional about key choices: what they're putting into their bodies; how the way they are spending their time helps them reach their larger purposes; who they're spending their time with; and what they're doing to contribute to their families, schools, and communities.

At the beginning of the school year and at each marking period, students in middle and high school should record in a journal their goals in these eight areas:

1. Academics
2. Social life
3. Sports and exercise
4. Healthy eating
5. Family and community
6. Hobbies and interests
7. Screen time
8. Long-term plans

In working with middle school students, for example, I have seen them set goals ranging from "eating better food at lunch" to "being a great guitar player" to "being an NBA star." In all cases, we want to help students be clear about their goals (in the first case, "to be a healthy person") and to set realistic short-term goals on the way to their long-term goal (for the guitar and basketball players, finding time for regular practice with feedback). For these students, and all students, goals provide anchors, especially valuable in high winds and rough seas.

Each of the eight areas of life above matter, and academic success is related to all of them. Having a way to focus on each of them separately, document progress, and create priorities is important. Students need help to be successful even when they have positive aspirations. A sure way to not succeed is trying to make progress in too many areas at once, so help students find one, two, or three areas to prioritize for a marking period. Revisit these priorities with them and see if follow-up goals need to be set in these areas or if new areas should be prioritized. Keeping to no more than three at a time is vital, because even if we might need to change in eight areas, we can't track that many. As you have heard before, slow and steady wins the race.

Tracking also helps ensure that a given area is not neglected. When we see that things might have been neglected, we can make some adjustments.

The main point of setting goals is to help students take realistic steps to achieve them. Many educators find that using the SMART format[6]—goals that are specific, measurable, attainable, relevant, and timely—is practical and reasonable, and keeps students on track.

## When Can This Happen?

This kind of journaling is ideally suited to advisory or extended homeroom periods. Advisory periods are supposed to focus on the whole child, and the eight areas provide broad coverage. Journaling also fosters communication between advisory teachers and those who focus on these areas in schools, including subject area teachers, "specials" teachers (including health and physical education teachers), and staff running extracurricular activities. In addition, the advisory period can be used for pair and group problem solving to help overcome obstacles students face as they pursue their goals.

One way to help students achieve their goals is to pair them up to help one another with goal setting and monitoring. Students see each other in various school contexts and can be helpful outside of formal class time.

Having communal, whole-class conversations about goal setting creates a new mindset in students and fosters cooperation and mutual improvement because students' goals are not solely their responsibility. We all get better when each of us gets better. So, there is an expectation that goals set will be shared—perhaps with classmates and certainly with relevant teachers. (This explicit expectation of sharing should ensure that personal goals related to family issues stay out of these conversations, as they require more professional and confidential follow-up.)

A helpful way to introduce the journaling is to ask students to reflect on the opening quote from Edison, taking a position as to whether they agree, disagree, or are not sure about it, and why. Have students share their rationales in small groups and then share out with the larger class. Ensuring that students understand they have more potential than most of them realize is a critical preliminary step to making goal journaling an authentic activity for them.

### The Same Goals Are Useful for Adults

This activity is also relevant for adults. Educators have a lot on their plates, and having a way to make sure that one's learning, family, health habits, interests, and long-term plans are front of mind (even if not always front of action) keeps us grounded.

Devoting regular time in professional learning communities and faculty meetings to discussing goal-achieving strategies can provide a power morale boost in schools. In particular, discussing long-term plans can stimulate broad faculty collaboration to shape the school. And sharing with students that you're doing the same thing you ask them to do makes it more likely that they'll value the activity.

## Building a Positive Mindset One Word at a Time

In her book, *The Days Between*,[7] Marcia Falk provides a set of words she uses to create poems about optimism and gratitude. What a marvelous activity for our students, to create a poem like that from the words she provides or that the teacher provides. This kind of activity can engage students in articulating a positive mindset, both individually and collectively.

**Writers' Workshop**
Ask your students to create a poem focused on a theme for social and emotional learning, or to create a story using these words, a subset of these words, or a related set of words—in the order the words are presented.

Here is Falk's positive word list (you will most likely want to include additional words):

- Abundant/abundance
- Blessings/blessing
- Beauty
- Creativity
- Confident/confidence
- Courageous/courage
- Calling/purpose
- Devoted/devotion
- Delight
- Enriched/enrichment
- Education
- Fulfillment
- Friendship/friend

- Grow/growth
- Good/goodness
- Health/healthiness
- Hope/hopefulness
- Included/inclusion
- Joy/joyfulness
- Kindness
- Love
- Music
- Nurturing
- Pleasure
- Peace/peacefulness
- Quiet/quietness
- Reason/reasonable
- Serene/serenity
- Solace
- Tolerance
- Truth/truthfulness
- Understanding
- Vision
- Wonder
- Yearnings/yearning
- Zeal

This writing activity is best done in student pairs or small groups. In whatever format you decide, create time for students to share what they've crafted. You can add a little entertainment and make the activity more challenging by assigning the groups to use only part of the list—A to H, I to P, or Q to Z, for example.

Be sure to thoroughly review the meaning of the list of positive words with students before they write. You can make the instructions for the poem more explicit, asking students to create a Poem of Aspirations or a Poem of Questions using the following stems (along with others you might brainstorm together):

- May we/May our...
- Why is/How can...
- Will I/Will we...

Here are some sample lines that use those stems:

- May we be inspired by joy, kindness, and love!
- Will I be courageous enough to listen to my calling?
- May we have the pleasure of peace and quiet in our lives.
- Why is there more comfort when we have tolerance for others?

Depending on the age and ability of your students, the list of words you provide will vary in complexity and length. (You may also choose to let them use the words in any order they wish and not in the order they are listed.)

With the set of words, students can also create a narrative of their school at its best. Options are always key in the classroom, so they could instead create a story about themselves at their best, or a classmate, friend, or family member. Consider providing them with story stems to assist them with starting their narratives. Simple stems are almost always best for getting those pens and pencils (or keyboards!) moving. Examples include: "It all started when...," "Few people know this, but...," and "At a young age..."

## Student Collaboration with Positive Word Play

Writing activities in which specific vocabulary words are provided help students build their language skills while also giving them a chance to use their creative voices. And as students share their creative products with each other—and with parents and perhaps other classrooms—you may find the conversation shifting in unexpectedly inspiring ways.

Additionally, as they collaborate with classmates, they are developing interpersonal competencies of respectful listening, taking turns, cooperation, and giving constructive feedback, while also building their social and emotional vocabularies.

Consider the opportunities you already have presented to your students for working together and sharing ideas around seeing themselves, each other, and life in a better, more positive light. The best of these will guide you in this set of activities, as well.

## Notes

1 https://news.gallup.com/poll/174785/americans-serving-communities-gain-edge.aspx#.U-pK7uNhqns.twitter
2 https://www.apa.org/pubs/journals/releases/fam-164381.pdf
3 http://www.columbia.edu/~im15/papers/hiclas.pdf
4 http://www.ascd.org/Publications/Books/Overview/The-Soul-of-Education.aspx
5 https://www.clal.org/
6 https://www.edutopia.org/blog/smart-goal-setting-with-students-maurice-elias
7 http://www.marciafalk.com/daysbetween.html

# 5

# Educational Approach D
# Promoting Sources of Inspiration and Human Dignity

The Reflection/Application Guide below is designed to help you bring the ideas in each of the practice-oriented examples into your professional practice. It is meant to serve as an advanced organizer. You may want to reproduce it to have available for note-taking as you read the various practice-oriented examples.

As you are reading the practice-oriented examples linked to each approach, consider the following questions:

1. Visualize how a specific idea you are reading about might fit into your classroom/practice context.
2. Reflect on how this is similar to or different from your current practice.
3. Write three or four specific ideas you can most readily apply from the practice-oriented examples in this section.

4. Ask the author a question that might help to clarify, adapt, extend your understanding, etc. (SECDLab@gmail.com).

## A Teaching Moment: The Peace Corps as a Source of Inspiration

Do you know how the Peace Corps got started? And do you know why it's important to know how? Let's take a moment to find the answers.

It started in 1961 with students greeting President John F. Kennedy at the University of Michigan for a 2 a.m. campaign rally. Spontaneously, he asked those in the raucous crowd of 10,000, that, among those who were planning to be doctors, "How many of you would be willing to spend your days in [the developing world] working for the US and working for freedom?" Their enthusiastic response led him to repeat this question to prospective technicians, teachers, and engineers. Each group was more enthusiastic than the next.

But the idea did not drop, as many campaign actions do. Eight hundred Michigan students signed petitions stating their intention to go overseas and these were presented to the Kennedy campaign. JFK proposed the idea of a Peace Corps at a speech in San Francisco just prior to the election, and the day after inauguration, he appointed Sargent Shriver to create this entity—for which many people volunteered after hearing the speech, but prior to its actual creation.

*Lesson #1*: Students at all levels, preschool through high school and college, respond to inspiration and a sense of higher purpose.

*Lesson #2*: All the goodwill in the world would have come to naught if Sargent Shriver had not set up an infrastructure to create a pathway from inspiration to action and if this structure did not live according to the ideals it espoused.

*Corollary for schools*: Our students need inspiration and then outlets to make a tangible difference. They will be willing to work for an opportunity like this. Service is a primary way, but not the only way, to make a difference in the lives of others. Sometimes it is just being able to share one's skills and gifts. But that must be organized and recognized.

## What are the Essential Principles of the Peace Corps That Can Be Part of the Climate of Classrooms and Schools?

There are no better words to express this than those of Sargent Shriver himself. Speaking at the 25th anniversary of the Peace Corps celebration[1] at a national conference of returned Peace Corps volunteers and staff in Washington DC on September 20, 1986, Shriver said:

> And we all think that everyone in the Peace Corps, and everyone who has ever worked in the Peace Corps, is a special person, who given a chance will overcome any problem! In believing this about each other, in believing this about all Peace Corps people, we are giving reality to the words of Martin Luther King, Jr.

*Lesson for schools*: Treat everyone in the school as special and everyone will be lifted up. Together, much can be done that cannot be accomplished by individuals alone.

> We cannot police the world. But we can begin to liberate it from despair and fear and anger by making economic development and mutual service the hard core of our foreign policy, and of our national defense!

*Lesson for schools*: Small steps, even amidst great despair, are the key to long-term and sustained success. Do not worry about aggrandizing yourself, and do not try to coerce. As we "liberate" students "from despair and fear and anger" by showing them possibilities for accomplishment and service that they might have only perceived dimly, if at all, we will find their willingness to work, learn, and achieve will blossom.

> I mean we are celebrating a happening, a movement, a reality which cannot be fully explained scientifically, mathematically, sociologically, or politically. A miracle transcends logic. Quantitative amassing of facts does not reveal its nature. Miracles, by definition, are inexplicable by normal human reasoning. They transcend ordinary reality. They surprise. They shock. They unsettle.

*Lesson for schools*: This is how climate changes. Classrooms and the school itself become the subject of a movement of liberation, improvement, meaning, and purpose. It is more than scores; it is transcendent. Anyone who has seen a classroom or school turn around, truly turn around, with heads held high and pride replacing dejection, knows exactly what Shriver is talking about.

> To believe in men and women, to believe they can surpass themselves, to believe that ordinary people can become extraordinary, to believe in young men and women, and know they can accomplish miracles—these were part of Kennedy's character and vision.

*Paraphrase for classrooms and schools*: To believe in teachers and other staff and students, to believe they can surpass themselves, to believe that ordinary can be turned into extra-ordinary, to believe in our students and to know that they can accomplish greatness—these are the essence of our vision for what all classrooms and schools can become.

Every anniversary of the Peace Corps is a time for inspiration. It is a time to realize that our potential is far greater than we typically believe and that we are held back less by our abilities than our circumstances and lack of structures enabling us to collaborate, cooperate, serve, learn, and soar. When Sargent Shriver was asked to create the Peace Corps, his first reaction was that he knew nothing about it and could not fathom how to create it.

But as he reflected again, he realized that the liberation of the human spirit, the channeling of hope into action, and learning skills to allow tangible contributions to the lives of others were things he did know about. And from those, the Peace Corps emerged and continues. And the same can happen in our most challenged classrooms and schools.

How might you use the story of the inception of the Peace Corps with students? What lessons are you already using to inspire caring for others and service in your students?

## A Tool to Encourage Students to Respect the Dignity of Their Classmates

No matter how hard we might try, the polarized climate outside of our classrooms still seeps into them. This climate pushes our students into us-versus-them thinking, toward less careful and open listening, and a higher degree of tension and anxiety from walking around in what can be a hostile environment due to relentless intimidation and bullying.

These conditions give rise to fearful exclusion of those unlike ourselves and, on rare but too frequent occasions, extremes of lashing out violently or ending one's own life in a desperate search for relief.

It's traditional to try to address these tendencies with healthy conflict resolution, communication, and effective relationship-building skills. But Tim Shriver,[2] cofounder of UNITE, an organization that supports national unity, believes that our attitudes and emotions direct our skills.

One of the attitudes and emotions that are far too prevalent is that of contempt. Tim Shriver (son of Sargent Shriver) has referred to contempt as a feeling of disdain and disgust for another person or group that is accompanied by an attitude of holding oneself above others and seeing others as worthless.

The opposite is dignity: seeing the inherent worth in everyone. An attitude of dignity counters polarization, promotes listening, and replaces hostility with caring.

A classroom or school that allows contempt to flourish—or even simmer—is the kind of place where students (and staff) experience fear when they should be focused on learning and on supporting one another. What's needed is a tool that can help classrooms and schools move away from contempt and toward dignity by shining the healing light of conversation.

The Dignity Index is a new measure created by UNITE in 2021[3] to help us better understand how we treat each other during disagreements. On this measure (ranging from 1 to 8), lower scores (1 and 2) indicate contempt and division, and higher scores (7 and 8) are indicative of someone who sees dignity in others, respects differences, and works together with others. Although this measure has not yet been brought to many schools, some have started.

Salt Lake City schools are using the Dignity Index in their classrooms. Here is an adaptation of what they have done:

8—Dignity: I treat everyone with dignity. I believe everyone is born with inherent value. Everyone is important and deserves to be treated with kindness and respect no matter who they are.

7—Connectedness: I fully engage with others. I listen and talk with people who have different ideas, even if I don't agree with them. I'm open to admitting mistakes I've made, and I am open to changing my opinion.

6—Curiosity: I make an effort to talk to a variety of other people, even if I don't agree with them on everything. I focus on our shared interests and common values.

5—Respect: I recognize that others have a right to be here and express their thoughts; even though it can be difficult, it's their school, too. We all belong here.

4—Dismissiveness: I'm better than them. They're different and annoying. They don't really belong. We shouldn't trust them.

3—Disdain: I'm doing as well as I can, while some others are responsible for so many problems here. We're the good people, and they're the bad people. It's us versus them.

2—Disgust: Some people here really disgust me. Things would be better if they weren't here. They're going to ruin everything if we let them. It's us or them.

1—Contempt: I hate some people in this school. They are terrible and are destroying it here. They need to go. They are not valuable humans. If we don't hurt them first, they will hurt us.

If your classroom or school does not feel comfortable and safe to you, it's likely that your ratings would be between 1 and 4. This implies that people are not listening to or talking patiently and caringly to one another. The developers of the index make the following suggestions to move up the Dignity Index.

## Improving Your Dignity Index

Guide people to use more dignity and less contempt in what they read, what they say, what they watch, and what they support.

Encourage people to expect the use of dignity from the people who represent them, entertain them, and inform them. This is how the culture can start to change.

There are two important parts to this suggestion. First, each of us in schools—and each of our students, especially starting at the secondary level—needs to adopt attitudes toward others that are characterized by more respect, curiosity, connectedness, and dignity. Second, we need to expect that those with whom we interact—as political leaders, entertainers and sports figures, and sources of our news and information—are not exemplars of dismissiveness, disdain, disgust, or contempt for others, generally or for particular groups.

## Put the Dignity Index to Work in Your Classroom

One activity is to take the eight words in the Salt Lake City version and present them to groups of students in mixed order and ask them to put them on a continuum, explaining the meaning of each word and why they created the order that they did. Have groups present their orders and discuss differences. You can have them create a composite version to use in your classroom/school. You also can present the Salt Lake City version and have them reflect on similarities and differences and/or use that version as a model to create a final version.

You might even want to have your class complete the Dignity Index on themselves periodically as a way to monitor the conversational climate. As you see your class's cumulative Dignity Index head toward a 7 or 8, you can proudly say that it has become a norm for your students to respect differences and work together.

Social and emotional learning skills underlie the need to treat others with dignity, and they are activated in the process of having genuine conversations.[4] Through conversations, we can help students build active listening skills, learn how to respectfully disagree with others, strengthen peer relationships, and support dignity. By creating our classrooms as safe, supportive spaces for critical and creative thinking and guiding students in how they talk to each other, we can improve their listening, learning, and character.

*What about you? As you reflect on your classroom and/or school, how do you think the concept of dignity can be used?*

## Maya Angelou's Poetry: A Lesson in Service, History, SEL, and Civics

Poetry is an essential part of the language arts curriculum. But it can be much more. Exposing our students to the powerful words and images of Maya Angelou's poetry builds their skills in reading, character education, vocabulary, civics, history, and humanity. Deeply exploring the topics and themes found in Angelou's poetry can inspire students, and even be life changing.

Below is an activity that can be used with students starting in the seventh grade, although it will be most appropriate for high school students. It's easily aligned with language arts standards and provides opportunities for building students' SEL skills in group work, leadership, communication, emotional awareness, empathy, and problem solving.

## The Lesson: Step by Step

Tell students that over the next few days, they will learn about Maya Angelou and her message. She composed a poem in 1995 for the 50th anniversary of the United Nations. Maya Angelou intended her poem to take concentration and focus to understand. Explain that this "may be one of the most difficult and important assignments you have ever had." Then, provide each student with a copy of her poem, "A Brave and Startling Truth," which you can find online.[5]

Step #1: Find a link online that will enable students to listen to Maya Angelou deliver the entire poem, or read it aloud to students. Have them read it again, silently.

Step #2: Explain to them that you've divided the poem into six parts:

> Part 1: Paragraph 1
> Part 2: Paragraphs 2 and 3
> Part 3: Paragraphs 4 and 5
> Part 4: Paragraphs 6 and 7
> Part 5: Paragraphs 8 and 9
> Part 6: Paragraphs 10 and 11

Place them into five small groups and assign each group to read one of the first five parts.

Step #3: Ask students to look up the words they don't know in the part that their group has been assigned.

Step #4: Have students work in their groups to figure out what their part means, writing down their thoughts and interpretations. Groups should pay special attention to the question linked to their part:

- Part 1: What do you think the brave and startling truth might be?

- Part 2: Who is the object of hostility, hate, and scorn?
- Part 3: What are some of the opposites Maya Angelou uses in Part 3 and what is the point she is trying to make? Is she being optimistic or pessimistic?
- Part 4: Why does she mention all of these natural wonders and how many of them had you heard of before now?
- Part 5: What is she saying about people? Is she being optimistic or pessimistic?

**Time for Class Discussion**

After each group has done its part, have each group present, in the order of the poem, the words they learned and then discuss the meaning of their section with the rest of the class.

After all the groups have presented, ask everyone to read Part 6 and think about the question for Part 6: What is the brave and startling truth that is the message of the poem and what does this have to do with the United Nations?

Follow by asking them what they think the brave and startling truth means for them, for their time in middle or high school, and their future.

## A Lesson About Cesar Chavez and Civil Rights

Open by saying the following (hand out or create a digital copy to help students better follow along):

### The Legacy of Cesar Chavez

We are going to learn about a man of great courage who believed that the most powerful weapon in the world was nonviolence and peace. His name was Cesar Chavez. I am going to read to you a little bit about his life. It's very important that you understand everything we are talking about. This is why we want you to learn to read and read well. If you can't read well, it's very hard to understand everything that is happening around you.

So, if you hear a word or an idea that you do not know, stop me and we will look it up. I also want you to learn how to look up what you don't know. Stop me as often as you need to. I know that there are many new words and difficult ideas ahead.

Cesar Chavez was a civil rights and labor leader, an advocate for farmworkers as well as a farmworker himself, and a champion of preserving our natural environment, especially from chemicals and pesticides. Chavez believed in nonviolence as a way to create social change. He and his followers used boycotts, strikes, and fasts as their methods.

Cesar Chavez was born in 1927 on a small farm near Yuma, Arizona. When he was 10 years old, his family's farm was taken over by the state because his family could not pay their bills. This led to his family traveling to various places to get jobs farming; they were what we now call migrant farm workers.

Adults and children worked 15 hours a day, every day, in the hot sun. They earned less than the minimum wage, sometimes a dollar an hour, sometimes less. They lived in rooms without bathrooms, with six to eight people per room. Cesar Chavez was one of many Mexican Americans living as migrant farm workers. They were known as Chicanos. Cesar Chavez, like most other Chicano migrant workers, attended more than 30 different elementary and middle schools growing up. They saw many signs that said "No dogs or Mexicans allowed" outside public places. He did not like this life and he did not like what he saw it doing to his family and others.

Many people do not know that ten years before Rosa Parks was arrested in Alabama for not giving up her seat on a bus, Cesar Chavez was arrested and put in prison in California because he sat in the section of a movie theater reserved for Japanese and white customers only, not for African Americans or Latinos. At that time, movie theaters were segregated.

Cesar Chavez led protests against the inhumane treatment of migrant workers and eventually of all workers who were underpaid, poorly treated, and exploited by their bosses. He worked with African Americans, Puerto Ricans, Filipinos, and Chicanos most of all, but not only. He taught them nonviolence and admired the methods of Martin Luther King, Jr. and Gandhi. He started an organization, the National Farm Workers Association, to serve as a union for workers and encouraged farm workers to work together and act together to be more effective. Strikes, boycotts, and marches led to many successes. He created great pride and dignity and hope in people.

Cesar Chavez once said, "When the man who feeds the world by toiling in the field is himself deprived of the basic rights of feeding and caring for his own family, the whole community of man is sick."

(Online you can find a brief audio of Cesar Chavez[6] telling a little about his life and accomplishments and featuring an example of his speaking about protests. Consider playing this for your class.)

## Time for Discussion

Below are parts of speeches by Cesar Chavez, one honoring the memory of Rev. Martin Luther King, Jr. after his assassination in 1968, and the other from the end of a fast that helped reduce the use of pesticides in grape farming in 1970.

Have students work in groups to read each part and look up the words, ideas, and places that they are not familiar with. You may want to start with the first paragraph of Part One for the whole group and model for them the importance of understanding everything they do not know and how to look up the information.

It will be very useful to spend time ensuring they understand the idea of a "rate" of such things as cancer and other health issues, and the importance of a community knowing how well or poorly the rates are in various areas. You might want to extend this at some point into a research project on health rates in the city or area where they live or suggest this as a follow-up project in math and/or science or health classes.

After they understand the words in each part, have them discuss the following questions, share their responses, and then have them go to the conclusion section:

## Excerpts from Chavez's Speeches
*Part One:*

> The Central Valley of California is one of the wealthiest agricultural regions in the world. In its midst are clusters of children dying from cancer. The children live in communities surrounded by the grape fields that employ their parents. The children come into contact with the poisons when they play outside, when they drink the water, and when they hug their parents returning from the fields. And the children are dying. They are dying slow, painful, cruel deaths in towns called cancer clusters, like McFarland, where the children's cancer rate is 800 percent above normal. ... Other young children are suffering from similar fatal diseases that the experts believe are caused by pesticides. These same pesticides can be found on the grapes you buy in the stores. My friends, the suffering must end. We have no choice, we have to stop the plague of pesticides.

*Part Two:*

> The growers responsible for this outrage are blinded by greed, by racism, and by power. The same inhumanity displayed at Selma, in Birmingham, in so many of Dr. King's battlegrounds, is displayed every day on the vineyards of California.

*Part Three:*

> The simple act of refusing to buy table grapes laced with pesticides is a powerful statement that the growers

understand. For your safety, for the workers, and for the children, we must act together. My friends, Dr. King realized that the only real wealth comes from helping others. I challenge you to carry on his work by volunteering to work for a just cause you believe in.

*Part Four:*

Our struggle is not easy. Those who oppose our cause are rich and powerful and they have many allies in high places. We are poor. Our allies are few. But we have something the rich do not own. We have our own bodies and spirits and the justice of our cause as weapons. When we are really honest with ourselves, we must admit that our lives are all that really belong to us. So, it is how we use our lives that determines what kind of people we are. It is my belief that only by giving our lives do we find life. I am convinced that the truest act of courage, the strongest act of manliness is to sacrifice ourselves for others in a totally nonviolent struggle for justice.

### Closing the Lesson
Tell the class, "Let's go back to what Cesar Chavez once said: 'When the man who feeds the world by toiling in the field is himself deprived of the basic rights of feeding and caring for his own family, the whole community of man is sick.'"

Then, arrange your students in small discussion groups and ask them to share their answers with the whole group to these questions:

- ♦ What do you think he meant by that?
- ♦ What basic rights do you feel you should have?
- ♦ Should everyone in the community or in school have those same rights? Why or why not?
- ♦ What can you do to help others have their rights?

Your students will emerge as changed and enlightened from this set of activities.

## Why Students Should Discover the Liberty Bell's True History

During the school year, where many students seem to know what's coming and don't always feel enthusiasm about it, there is value in asking all of upper elementary and secondary students to think about something most will have heard of, but not thought about in detail. Why? Because ultimately, education is about looking more deeply at the world around us—especially parts of the world we have noticed but not thought about deeply. Education is about asking insightful and focused questions and creating new knowledge, not simply accepting what is being presented.

The Liberty Bell is a great vehicle for project-based learning that can create a common conversation in the school that guides students to look more deeply into what they are learning. We want them to be curious learning detectives!

### In the Classroom

There are two assignments below that can be modified according to your time, goals, and wider curricular requirements. I suggest treating this as an informal competition, with students being given latitude, or constraints, on how to present their results, depending on other educational priorities you might want to address. For example, student teams might create posters for a Liberty Bell Exposition in the school auditorium one evening, inviting parents and the community.

There might be debates set up during lunch periods, where teams present their positions and are challenged by other teams, who then present their own positions, and so on. Or small groups of students may work on this in a class on language arts, history/social studies, civics, character, or research skills, and present to one another. Ultimately, some consensus on the "true" story should be reached—even if it is that there is not a single, "true" story. This consensus can be presented in written, video, visual and performing arts-related, or other formats.

## Post-Activity Reflection Is Essential

Regardless of the approach and the specifics of the assignment, be sure to ask each participant to reflect on the experience of working in the team, what they learned personally about their own style of being in a team, what was frustrating, what was enlightening, how decisions were made (such as what and how many sources to consult, what format would be used for presenting), and any other reflections they would like to share. In this way, the activity is reinforcing social-emotional and character development and its integration with academic content.

## Assignment #1: The Liberty Bell

Directions: Create a history of the Liberty Bell using at least three different (non-AI) sources. Be sure to address these questions in your response:

- How many Liberty Bells have there been?
- What is the quotation on the Liberty Bell and where did it come from? Who chose it and why? What other translations are there of that quote? What part of the quote was omitted? What would be changed by adding it?
- How did the Liberty Bell get its name?
- What note was the Liberty Bell intended to sound?
- What is the modern history of the Liberty Bell—who has used it as a symbol, either physically or in writing or speeches? Why did they choose this as a symbol?
- What are the lessons we can learn today from the history of the Liberty Bell?

Responses to the final question can cover the need to be careful in one's work, the importance of having ideals/purposes and attempting to live up to them, the value and meaning of symbols, the importance of collaboration, courage, and leadership, the meaning of freedom and liberty in revolutions then and now, the challenges in finding the "truth" of what happened in a situation, or the benefits of understanding the context of a quote.

**Assignment #2: A Biographical Investigation**
Directions: Who was Jacob Duché and what was his role in the American Revolution? (Be sure to use at least three different, non-AI sources.) Be sure to address these questions in your response:

- What did Duché do that would have led people to refer to him as a person of inspiration? As a person of courage? As a traitor? What is your opinion of him?
- What was Duché's relationship with George Washington?
- What title did Duché have after the Declaration of Independence? What title did Duché have in England?

Be creative in finding ways for your students give one another constructive feedback or comments and to share their investigations with other classes, at a presentation for parents, and/or highlight on your school's website.

# Notes

1 https://www.sargentshriver.org/archive/speeches/speech-at-the-national-conference-of-returned-peace-corps-volunteers-and-staff
2 https://www.dignityindex.us/tim-shriver
3 https://www.dignityindex.us/index
4 https://resources.corwin.com/morningclassroomconversations
5 https://www.themarginalian.org/2018/05/09/a-brave-and-startling-truth-maya-angelou/
6 http://www.freedomarchives.org/audio_samples/Mp3_files/Cesar_Chavez_in_English.mp3

# 6

# Educational Approach E
# Articulating Personal Values and Sense of Positive Purpose

The Reflection/Application Guide below is designed to help you bring the ideas in each of the practice-oriented examples into your professional practice. It is meant to serve as an advanced organizer. You may want to reproduce it to have available for note-taking as you read the various practice-oriented examples.

As you are reading the practice-oriented examples linked to each approach, consider the following questions:

1. Visualize how a specific idea you are reading about might fit into your classroom/practice context.
2. Reflect on how this is similar to or different from your current practice.
3. Write three or four specific ideas you can most readily apply from the practice-oriented examples in this section.

4. Ask the author a question that might help to clarify, adapt, extend your understanding, etc. (SECDLab@gmail.com).

## Helping Your Students Identify Their Values

The beginning of the school year is a good time to ask students to reflect on what gives them guiding direction in their lives. And writing their guiding principles for life is a perfect assignment for doing so.

For teachers of students fifth grade and up, ask your students to describe the laws by which they want to live their life. To help them get the idea, discuss any biographies they have read or watched (or watch clips or TED Talks about the careers and interests of individuals from various walks of life to whom your students will relate) and then discuss or list together a summary of the rules by which these individuals seemed to live their lives. Also ask students the same question about characters in novels, artists, scientists, or historical figures, depending on what you have studied or are studying with them.

### Getting Started

Question prompts will help students start thinking more deeply about their own values or principles:

- Whom do you admire? List three of that person's admirable qualities.
- Describe an incident or event from which you learned a lesson "the hard way."
- What could you change about yourself to become a better person?
- What three qualities do you value in a friend? A teacher? A parent?

- Who has been most important in your life in helping you establish your values? Please explain.
- What are the three most important values you think it will be important to encourage in your children one day?
- What is the one rule that you believe is important to live your life by?
- If we lived in a perfect world, how would people behave differently than they do now?

You may find it useful to have each student write their own answers to some or all of the prompts first and then ask students to share these in pairs, with a segment of a class, or in a whole-class discussion.

Teachers should follow up students' statements with questions to help them think more deeply about their answers. For example: What makes these qualities worth admiring and worth following? How did you choose that particular incident or example or person? Why are these qualities or values so important to you?

### Crafting a Reflective Essay

After students have had a chance to think about and discuss the prompts, they will be ready to start to write. A reflective essay of this sort can be linked in format to students' appropriate grade-level language arts writing standards and objectives. Instruct them to reflect on the past year, both in and out of school, and write about what they consider to be the values or principles by which they want to live their lives, and why.

In my work with teachers who have guided students through this task, the resulting essays were moving, revealing, and inspiring. Students have often told stories about family members and important events in their lives. They have addressed such themes as love, responsibility, respect, relationships, perseverance, self-discipline, courage, honesty, and kindness—and often in combination.

One student, writing about how he and his siblings were about to be removed from their home by child protective services following the arrest of their mother, described how their mother's friend, whom they had never met, fought for legal custody of them when no other family member appeared. His law of life was the importance of giving love even to people he does not know. Another student wrote: "I think loving others is the most important. A person must have love in his or her life. Love makes a person feel important."

Here is part of an eighth-grader's essay about perseverance:

> The key to success in my life is perseverance. My purpose is to continue to reach my goals, despite difficulties that I may face. My great grandmother was a person who struggled to make sure her family would be successful. Born in 1902, she was a maid who worked extremely hard just to make ends meet. She walked miles to get to work because she didn't have money for transportation; after working in someone's kitchen all day, she came home to take in laundry. Her driving desire to make life better for her children and theirs motivated her to persevere in a time when being black meant you were considered less than nothing.
> (Excerpted from *Urban Dreams: Stories of Hope, Resilience, and Character.*)[1]

## Moving from Reflection to Application

Once you engage students in this essay writing, ask them to commit themselves to living by their principles or laws thereafter. Throughout the rest of the school year, you can have them reflect on what they wrote and committed to, check in with you or with designated peers on how they are doing on following through, and revise their principles (or behaviors) as necessary.

## Guiding Students in Finding Their Truth

What is your students' relationship with truth? It may seem like an odd question (or perhaps not, depending on your current context), but knowing your middle and high school students' relationship to the truth may tell you a lot about their character and their path to future success.

In his book about the last year of the life of Martin Luther King, Jr. titled *Death of a King: The Real Story of Dr. Martin Luther King Jr.'s Final Year*,[2] Tavis Smiley focuses on what it means to be truthful.

Martin Luther King, Jr. had opinions about segregation, education, housing, and local, state, and federal laws. He also had opinions about how people should live together and treat one another.

Tavis Smiley felt that one of the most distinctive characteristics of Dr. King was his relationship to the truth. He always tried to ally with the truth. Of course, he also knew that others disagreed with him, believing in other truths.

### In the Classroom

So, what does Tavis Smiley suggest we can do for our young people?

*1. Have a conversation with them about how they know when something is true.*

This should include things they read, internet information (including photos), things they learn from media sources, and things they believe about other people and about relationships.

A related conversation is about the values they hold most closely. Books like *Urban Dreams: Stories of Hope, Resilience, and Character* help teens think about their values by reading about peers' values, and how and why they came to hold them.

*2. Present these four aspects of truth and discuss them with your students.*

1. Seek. You have to seek the truth. You can't assume it's coming your way. Many people want to get you to agree with them and hold their opinions, but it's not necessarily the truth. You also have to feel the truth is right. If you have doubts, continue to seek.
2. Speak. Once you believe something is true, you have to communicate it clearly. That's why it becomes so important to have good writing and speaking skills, as Martin Luther King, Jr. did. If you can't express your ideas in ways that people can understand, the truth is not being well served.
3. Stand By. Know how to defend your point of view. Avoid peer pressure, which is really following other people's goals for you, instead of acting according to your own goal and values. Act like an upstander for your beliefs, especially with your peers. It takes courage, but this is what it means to be a person of character.
4. Stay With. People who are always shifting their point of view and values lack integrity. Tell your students the following: Your problem-solving skills and ability to overcome obstacles are important. Your values matter, too, but don't be afraid to reevaluate them. However, this must be serious. You can't shift just because there is some questioning. Think it through and do what makes the most sense to you.

*3. Spread the truth. Encourage students to know that if you believe it, share it.*

Martin Luther King, Jr. wrote a famous and important letter from the Birmingham jail. Ask your students to read it and ask them why they think he wrote it. Help them see that it was not enough for Dr. King to know and believe the truth. It had to be spread to others.

### Setting the Historical Context

The March on Washington for Jobs and Freedom in 1963 similarly required extensive communication, not only about the march itself but also about the principles of nonviolence that had to govern the marchers, regardless of provocation. If the truth were only held by a select few, our nation would be a very different place today. This will also lead to a discussion about how individuals differ about the truth.

Those who supported segregation believed (and, sadly, still believe) in the truth of separation of races. This is another reason to follow the four aspects of truth and to spread what you believe, when you believe it strongly, while being respectfully open to, and analytical about, disagreement. Introducing the Dignity Index to students as part of this overall conversation about truth can provide a structure for how to handle disagreements (see Chapter 5).

Talking to your students about truth can help build their values and, most of all, their sense of integrity. That is a quality that will serve them well in college, careers, and relationships.

## Helping Students Find Purpose and Appreciation for School

In a popular *New York Times* article titled "Why You Hate Work,"[3] Tony Schwartz and Christine Porath identify four areas that matter most to job satisfaction and productivity:

1. Feeling good and recharged physically.
2. Feeling like an appreciated and valued contributor.
3. Having a clear focus and a say in prioritizing.
4. Seeing a higher purpose in the work.

Think about how this applies to your job situation. The prediction of Schwartz and Porath would be that to the extent you feel these four areas are strongly true for you in your work in school, you will like your job and look forward to getting there in the morning. On the other hand, if these areas are not true for you, then you will be more reluctant to head to school and you are also more likely to feel job-related stress.

Sadly, for too many educators, the glass is closer to 25 percent full than 90 percent full. The COVID 19 pandemic and its aftermath have elevated already high levels of workplace stress. During the course of the school year, a whirling crescendo of test-driven anxiety increases relentlessly until the conclusion of the last makeup test. When the test scores finally arrive, it is, in many ways, anticlimactic because there are usually no surprises; one often can't work directly with one's own students who were tested based on the results, and staff and administrative changes are not uncommon.

### Considering Our Students

Now step back for a moment and look at the four areas and apply them to your students. If we did a parallel, "Why You Hate School," then shortcomings in the four areas would also explain a lot.

Where to begin? One thing I have learned from work with many schools over many years is that steps toward improvement must be taken one at a time. If you and your students have shortcomings in all four areas mentioned earlier, you cannot correct them all at once in a lasting and deep way. You will have to be selective. It hardly matters where to start, as long as you realize that you need to start at the same place for both educators and students.

Changes need not be dramatic. Small things done over 180 school days add up to make a big difference. Here are some ideas for starting points in the four areas for you and your students:

**Recharge**: Insert short breaks for physical activity—stretching, dancing, jumping, or walking around. Provide regular times for reflection, which also has recharging value.

**Appreciation**: Compliment your colleagues on the small things they do. Don't overly praise—just noticing and commenting appreciatively is quite powerful. Similarly, for students, lower your threshold for showing your gratitude. Catch them being good when they are sitting still, following instructions, walking appropriately in the hallways, helping other students, speaking in a respectful tone of voice, being creative.

**Ownership:** Think about what you value most in the lessons you are covering and be sure to emphasize that and communicate that to your students. Where possible, give your students choice about what to do first, perhaps different ways to complete an assignment, whom to work with, how to end the school day. If you do more of this even once per week, it will be a great contrast to existing practices and make a difference to your students. And if you can do it more often, so much the better.

**Purpose:** Remind yourself about why you went into education. Have conversations about this with your colleagues. Look at your school's mission statement, annual goals, motto, and focal values and try to bring them more to life. Use some common planning time to discuss the big picture with your colleagues and how what you are doing benefits your students regardless of whether it shows up on the test score results. Talk about how you can improve your impact on students, collaboratively.

### Next Steps

With your students, discuss their aspirations and your aspirations for them. Help them see a positive future. Refuse to believe that they cannot succeed in college, careers, community, and family. Allow them to air their hesitations and balance that with your view of their destiny to make positive contributions. Sir John Templeton once said that "Every useful life is a ministry," and that every life can be a useful life.

By ministry, he was not invoking religion. Rather, he was invoking the idea of living for a purpose, ideally a Noble Purpose. This is a message your students need to hear often, and if they start to believe it, they will be more willing to do the work to learn the skills needed for that ministry. And then, both you and your students will find more joy and inspiration in work and in school.

## Developing a Sense of Purpose

When students enter the schoolhouse without a sense of positive purpose, it is difficult for them to connect their varied learning experiences and other opportunities into a coherent whole that shapes their lives. Without a purpose, they may lack a strong reason to learn, to take on challenges, or to behave well. An enduring sense of purpose typically emerges in adulthood but having a primary goal or a focus on something other than, and larger than, oneself and acting in alignment with these beliefs start to become particularly important in middle school.

Stanford University psychologist William Damon views purpose as a "stable and generalized intention to accomplish something that is at once meaningful to the self and of positive consequence to the world beyond the self."

Not surprisingly, positive purpose is connected to social and emotional learning (SEL) skills:

- You recognize your feelings and use them as a guide to your actions.
- You find your special task—what it is that allows you to excel.
- You appreciate your achievements and those of others, both large and small, as they contribute to a positive purpose.

### Getting Started with a Positive Purpose Essay

Writing an essay about positive purpose is an important way to build social awareness, as well as to provide direction and energy for learning. But students usually can't just start writing such an essay on their own—you need to help them build up to it:

1. Look at the positive purpose of well-known individuals. Use nonfiction books, biographies, documentaries, social studies texts, and news reports to get students thinking.
2. Have them learn about, reflect on, and write about the positive purpose of someone they know, or know of, by interviewing several from among a local hero, community leader, member of the clergy, first responder, family member, or educator or other staff member in the school.
3. Have them write about their own positive purpose.

### Use a Prompt to Guide Writing

You can use a grade-level-appropriate writing prompt suited to your students' ability, and adapt it so that a positive purpose is the subject of the essay. Here is a prompt example from a middle school in Jersey City, New Jersey:

> In your classes and in your life, you may have learned about and encountered people with a strong sense of purpose. Similarly, you might feel your own sense of purpose. In a five-paragraph essay that includes an introduction, three body paragraphs, and a conclusion, please respond to the following: What is your definition of purpose? What might be your purpose? Why? How would someone know that is your purpose in life?

The following are excerpts from an essay written by an eighth-grader based on the prompt above. (The student's school is located in a high-poverty area of Jersey City, and the school has been deemed low achieving by the state.)

Here is her introduction and definition of *purpose*:

> "The purpose of human life is to serve, and to show compassion and the will to help others," said Albert

Schweitzer. I believe I was made to entertain, inspire creativity, and guide others.

I think the definition of purpose means reason to do something, like when you say what's your purpose for choosing a certain career, and you state your reasons. This is why I strongly am convinced that I was made to guide and entertain others because, having a strong passion for art and Broadway plays... A purpose of doing something can lead you into realizing what you want to grow up to be, as you recognize what you like to do.

In the same essay, she responded to the prompt question, "How would someone know that is your purpose in life?"

Others would realize what my purpose in life is by knowing what my career and life goals are or, who I admire to be one day. I admire to be like Steve Jobs because I believe without mistakes you can never grow to be an exemplary person and, even though Steve Jobs failed many times he became one of the most successful men in our generation.

## Try It with Your Students

The student's essay opened her teacher's eyes to the depth of her thinking, aspirations, and abilities. The teacher reported that many of the student's classmates also produced insightful essays.

Aside from an essay, there are other ways in which your students can communicate their positive purpose. Consider how they might do this through artistic renderings other than writing—with visual art or music, for example.

If you decide to embark with your students on the essay assignment, I recommend that as they write, you provide a space for them to share early drafts of their essays with classmates to get several rounds of feedback, and then practice reading aloud in small groups. And then take a powerful next step: Provide them an opportunity to share in front of the class, or at an assembly, or at a parent or community gathering. Making their positive purpose public is a wonderful way to celebrate the inspirations and aspirations of your students and help catalyze them into action.

## Notes

1 https://www.bloomsbury.com/us/urban-dreams-9780761838432/
2 https://www.hachettebookgroup.com/titles/david-ritz/death-of-a-king/9780316332774/
3 http://www.nytimes.com/2014/06/01/opinion/sunday/why-you-hate-work.html

# 7

# Educational Approach F
# Cultivating an Attitude of Gratitude

The Reflection/Application Guide below is designed to help you bring the ideas in each of the practice-oriented examples into your professional practice. It is meant to serve as an advanced organizer. You may want to reproduce it to have available for note-taking as you read the various practice-oriented examples.

As you are reading the practice-oriented examples linked to each approach, consider the following questions:

1. Visualize how a specific idea you are reading about might fit into your classroom/practice context.
2. Reflect on how this is similar to or different from your urrent practice.
3. Write three or four specific ideas you can most readily apply from the practice-oriented examples in this section.

> 4. Ask the author a question that might help to clarify, adapt, extend your understanding, etc. (SECDLab@gmail.com).

## Habits of the Heart: Helping Students Reflect and Act on Gratitude

Gratitude no longer has to be reserved for special occasions and amazing circumstances. Researchers, led by the National Association of School Psychologists (NASP) along with Robert Emmons and Jeffrey Froh, have shown that there are benefits to expressing gratitude, even to "counting one's blessings." But doing so takes a bit of practice.

### Classroom Activities

What follows are some practical ways you can have students reflect on and express gratitude:

*Thank You Cards*

Ask students to think of someone in the school who has been helpful to them in some way, large or small, to whom they would like to thank, or express extra thanks. For younger students, you may have to help them think of some different groups of people to consider—teachers, office staff, custodians, kitchen staff, transportation workers, school support staff, and aides. Have students write and/or draw a card that communicates their appreciation for that help. Once completed, arrange for these to be delivered within the school, ideally by the children. Afterwards, discuss as a group how it felt to write to these various people.

*Appreciation Journals*

Ask students to keep journals in which they make practice-oriented entries each day about things big or small that they appreciate. This can be coordinated with language arts curricula, in that they can be asked to use different writing styles, sentence lengths, vocabulary, etc. to express themselves. Have them review their journals periodically and, ideally, share with one or two classmates. Help students expand the everyday occurrences for which they feel a sense of gratitude.

*Where Did That Come From?*
In conjunction with ongoing curriculum emphases, pick common objects that you are studying and ask the question, "Where did that come from?" or the related question, "How did that get here?" A good example is an apple. Work backward with your students (using the Internet or other sources when necessary) to trace the path that led that apple to find its way from a seedling to your school. Other common items—chalk, markers, a ruler, a piece of paper, a musical instrument, a piece of sports equipment—can be traced back to their origins so that students can develop a sense of appreciation for the many things that had to happen to bring these objects to your school, and to them. Of course, this concept can be extended into the content of ANY school subject area!

*Gratitude Poster/Gratitude Board*
Put a Gratitude Poster/Gratitude Board in your room that students can write on. You can have a different gratitude-related theme each month or you can alternate between two themes, for example: "Things We Are Grateful For" and "We Did It!" The first theme is about basic gratitude, and it provides the opportunity to broaden students' appreciation for people and things that affect their lives. The second theme is a listing of something a student accomplished *and* the names of one or more people who helped them to be successful. We want students to recognize the truth of the statement that in success, we stand on one another's shoulders. This does not take away from students' success, but in fact adds to it. Two examples: "I got a B+ on my test because my sister let me study" and "I learned a solo in a song in chorus because Thomas practiced with me."

*Gratitude Reflection*

NASP has a number of resources to help bring a variety of gratitude approaches into schools, as well as connecting to the home.

One activity that NASP recommends is a process of reflecting on gratitude. Have students consider the following:

- Why this good thing happened.
- What this good thing means to you.
- What you can do tomorrow to enable more of this good thing.
- What you learned from taking the time to name this good thing.
- What ways you or others contribute to this good thing.

## The Rationale

When we promote gratitude in our students—and in our own children—we are giving them a great gift. What we understand about the effects of gratitude is similar to what we understand about the benefits of giving up grudges and more generally embracing a stance of greater appreciation. Dwelling in negative emotions—including selfish emotions—is not the optimal state for learning, growth, or well-being. One of the reasons why writing about trauma is so effective is that it helps dispel or reframe the negative emotions involved.

It does not and cannot change unfortunate and sometimes tragic events. But it can help shift perspective toward greater positive engagement with others and with life. Just as writing about trauma is valuable, so is writing about gratitude.

How do you practice and teach gratitude in your classroom with your students?

## SEL and Lessons in Forgiveness and Gratitude

There are many instances in which ancient wisdom anticipated contemporary research, and one of them can be found on the

Jewish observance day of Yom Kippur. It is also known as the Day of Atonement, and it is considered the holiest day in the Jewish calendar.

Why? Without being overly technical or detailed, Yom Kippur represents the last day, the last time a person can review their deeds from the prior year and ask forgiveness for the regrettable things they have done. If one does not do so, there is the risk of harsh Divine judgment for the upcoming year. Of course, you are asking yourself, what if I did something that was not intended to hurt or insult others, that I did not realize required atonement? The Jewish liturgy of Yom Kippur has taken that into account. One is able to ask for forgiveness of both intentional and unintentional offenses, as well as those one is aware of committing and those one is unaware of that took place.

If one were to remove all religious connotations, there would still be much benefit to be derived from a guaranteed period of time to review the prior year's potential transgressions. But the Jewish tradition asks more of us, and this aligns with research. Yom Kippur is not the Day of Regret—it's the Day of Atonement.

**The History and Research**
The word atonement derives from $16^{th}$ century Latin and means unity or reconciliation; another common meaning was reparation or expiation from sin. Atonement involves something that we now associate with forgiveness: it is an active process. Indeed, true forgiveness is an active, intentional process that results in a genuine emotional change toward the person or event that was previously viewed as harmful, hurtful, hateful, or humiliating.

As you might infer, the Jewish sages' concept of atonement was really comprehensive forgiveness—for transgressions committed to others, to one's deity, or even to oneself. Holding on to strong negative feelings was viewed as harmful; actively finding release from those feelings was seen as beneficial. Thus, religious services were designed to provide that relief if it did not happen in any other way, though the likelihood of genuine emotional change through prayer could not be guaranteed.

Research suggests that forgiveness has been associated with lowered levels of anxiety, depression, stress, and anger, as well as greater compassion for others and appreciation of one's social support. Some believe that atonement and forgiveness can produce insights that can lead to a renewed sense of meaning and purpose in life. Most research on the relationship of forgiveness and well-being has been carried out with adults, but findings with adolescents have been similar.

## What Does This Have to Do with Social, Emotional, and Character Development?

The message here is that forgiveness is an essential part of any classroom management and school climate strategy. Students who engage in harmful actions toward others should be required to seek forgiveness. Both apologies and compensatory actions can be invoked. This may seem contradictory; how can genuine emotional change result from a forced process? Consider this: first, for the victim, being able to grant forgiveness is reassuring and strengthening. Second, for the perpetrator, being granted forgiveness, even if one is not sincere in the apology, can be liberating. It might not be, but it can be.

Finally, when two individuals have been involved in a negative situation, having a process of mutual forgiveness allows both to move on. There are no guarantees here, any more than attending a religious service can definitely produce emotional change. But it creates the potential for change to occur. Of course, having social-emotional competencies is essential for dealing effectively with all interpersonal situations, including those that might engender the need for forgiveness and how the forgiveness process is handled.

Frederic Luskin, a leader in forgiveness interventions, teaches individuals how to reframe negative life experiences and value gratitude in one's life, to shift one's attention more toward the positive. This allows victims to focus less on their role of victim, expend less emotional and psychological energy on blaming the offender, and move beyond the unfortunate events that have occurred in their lives. This can be especially useful when there is no perpetrator with whom to reconcile, and/or when the relevant incidents are in the past and not capable of being changed.

Forgiveness has some controversy to it. Might victims of social injustices be less inclined toward social action if they were more inclined toward forgiveness? Would schools stop seeing bullying as an organizational and climate problem and instead rely on forgiveness as a mechanism for bully response? Could insincere apologies lead to unwarranted second chances? Perhaps, if forgiveness were to be the sole value used to guide all moral decision making and action. But it's not. Schools, classrooms, and families are—or should be—oriented toward prevention of actions that otherwise might require forgiveness.

That said, the takeaway message from Yom Kippur is that forgiveness—and its close cousin, gratitude—is an important part of everyday life and has a place in the routines of classrooms and schools.

(Some of the information in this piece was drawn from Cydney Van Dyke Terreri, whom I thank for her many insights about forgiveness.)

*Additional information on forgiveness and youth*
Van Dyke, C. J., & Elias, M. J. (2007). How forgiveness, purpose, and religiosity are related to the mental health and well-being of youth: A review of the literature. *Mental Health, Religion & Culture, 10*(4), 395–415.
Terreri, C. J., & Elias, M. J. (2010). Forgiveness. In R. J. R. Levesque (Ed.), *Encyclopedia of Adolescence.* Springer.

## Gratitude Builds Character and Health

If your family is like most families, you took a few moments on Thanksgiving to give thanks for your food, the company of those around the table, and for the good things that happened in the past year. Many of you did this even though it may have not been such a good year, and perhaps you lost people who had been around the table only a year ago, so full of life.

Be assured that this simple act of gratitude is being shown by more and more research to be very healthy for you and for those around you. It's not a vaccination; doing it once a year does not provide the most health benefits. Expressing gratitude is like taking a daily vitamin. Its health benefits require consistency and repetition to yield maximum effect.

Don't take my word for it! Researchers like Robert Emmons, Martin Seligman, Monica Bartlett, and David DeSteno, as well as studies funded by the John Templeton Foundation, have found that keeping a daily gratitude journal, showing appreciation when others give you even minor help, and delivering overdue gratitude to someone who helped you a long time ago all have beneficial effects; those expressions of gratitude that directly involve others often move them to be more appreciative of and helpful to the next people they may meet.

Your gratitude must be genuine, but it need not be earthshaking. Thanking someone for listening to you, for how they prepare food, or for how they tell a story, or noting in your gratitude journal small things for which you are grateful that you might otherwise take for granted (such as a comfortable chair, the way the sunlight enters your room in the morning, or for the energy to get up and start exercising) all can make a positive difference in your life and the lives of those for whom you are grateful.

### A Clear Message for Teachers

For teachers, the message is clear: Don't be stingy with your appreciation. Show gratitude for things you "expect" to happen, such as children putting their things where they are supposed to, paying attention, sitting relatively quietly, asking good questions, helping classmates, turning in their homework on time, reading or speaking clearly in class. You will find that these actions will become much more contagious, and your students will feel better about themselves and being in school. Note that expressions of gratitude are not the same as praise. They are personal statements from you to your students saying how their actions help you and/or the class in some tangible way.

Giving thanks on Thanksgiving has character and mental health benefits that can be greatly extended as we make the expression of gratitude a regular part of our daily lives—and integrate it into school life as well.

## Holidays or Holy Days: Strategies for Teaching About Celebrations

December is a season of celebrations, whether it's Christmas, Chanukah, Kwanzaa, commemorations that are linked to the lunar calendar, such as the Islamic observance of Fatemiyeh, or Diwali, which often comes up in November. It's safe to say that most of the world's population is taking time to remember some influential historic events during this time period, and to commemorate them.

For this reason, in every elementary school classroom, and language arts and social studies-related classes in secondary schools, a few moments should be taken for class discussion about celebrations. Here are some questions that can guide the discussion. Some will be more developmentally and situationally appropriate than others and some will require adjustment:

- What does it mean to celebrate?
- What are some things your family celebrates at this time of year (it's fine if students mention personal celebrations, such as a parent's birthday, though the goal is to get at more cultural/religious celebrations)?
- Can you think of someone you know that celebrates something different from you and your family around this time of year? Why do they celebrate it?
- What are some different ways to celebrate? Are celebrations always happy? (Here, you want to encourage acknowledging

that some events are celebrated, or remembered, in ways that can be sad; sometimes celebrations are quiet and involve emotionally meaningful actions, such as laying a wreath or flowers on a commemorative location.)
- Why do so many different people and groups celebrate things?
- What's the most important part of celebrations? (Here, you want to encourage all responses—food, fun, being with family, remembering important things, stories, rituals, gifts, music, appreciation, gratitude—while making the point that one should always be sure to understand what is being celebrated and keep it in mind.) Consider supplementing this lesson with stories about celebrations. You can have students go to the Internet to learn about one kind of celebration they heard about from classmates that they did not know about and do a brief project on it.

You can have students interview family members about past family celebrations. In social studies and civics classes, there is opportunity to explore national and civic celebrations, historical celebrations that may not in fact still occur, as well as others that are relatively new. Mentioning national and local monuments as part of celebrations can be interesting and lead to useful Internet research. Art and music classes afford opportunities to see and hear the products of celebrations of various kinds.

Ultimately, you would like to make the point that it is in our nature to celebrate, and that people everywhere always take time to remember important people and events. That does not mean we should only think about these things once per year, or whatever the celebration period is. The celebration is to make sure we don't go too long without remembering and, usually, involves coming together with others who share the meaning of the celebration with us.

Celebrations are part of the way in which we learn to be emotionally intelligent and promote our students' social-emotional and character development.

# 8

# Educational Approach G

# Developing Students' Intrinsic Motivation and Engagement

The Reflection/Application Guide below is designed to help you bring the ideas in each of the practice-oriented examples into your professional practice. It is meant to serve as an advanced organizer. You may want to reproduce it to have available for note-taking as you read the various practice-oriented examples.

As you are reading the practice-oriented examples linked to each approach, consider the following questions:

1. Visualize how a specific idea you are reading about might fit into your classroom/practice context.
2. Reflect on how this is similar to or different from your current practice.
3. Write three or four specific ideas you can most readily apply from the practice-oriented examples in this section.

> 4. Ask the author a question that might help to clarify, adapt, extend your understanding, etc. (SECDLab@gmail.com).

## How and Why Intrinsic Motivation Works

We are more aware than ever that student motivation and engagement are essential for lasting learning. But there is less discussion of how and why intrinsic motivation works. In fact, when we talk about "motivating students," we lose sight of the fact that they are *already* motivated—just often not to do what educators want them to do! That's why understanding intrinsic motivation is so important. We need to work with students' motivational systems more than impose motivation from the outside (i.e., extrinsically).

### Deci and Ryan on Intrinsic Motivation

There is an intrinsic need for personal autonomy, self-determination, and to feel that one is choosing one's behavior, versus being controlled externally. The work of Edward Deci and William Ryan, *Why We Do What We Do: Understanding Self-Motivation*,[1] has been the exemplar in elaborating on the importance of what has come to be called "intrinsic motivation."

Choice is an essential element in feeling a sense of control. But when choices are offered, individuals need to have the information necessary for making a meaningful decision, not simply choosing between unclear options. Children also don't benefit much from choice when there likely are constraints after a choice is made. Notice the difference between #1 and 2, and #3 and 4.

1. What kind of book would you like to read?
2. What would you like to do at recess?
3. Do you want to focus on the Battle of Vicksburg or what happened at Antietam?

4. Do you want to show what you learned by writing an essay, writing out an interview script, or writing the script for a video documentary?

To generate more visible enthusiasm, as well as compliance under less monitoring, try to give instructions in autonomy-supportive ways, versus conventional, controlling ways:

**Example:** Cleanup by young children after an art project

- **Controlling:** "Keep the materials neat; don't mix up the colors; don't get any paint on the floor; be sure your smocks stay on."
- **Supportive:** "I know sometimes it's fun to slop the paint around, but we need to keep the materials and the room nice for the other children who will use them."

This, of course, may seem familiar as Diana Baumrind's empirically supported "authoritative" approach to parents speaking with children. That approach includes a rationale they can understand for why a limit is being set.

## Giving Corrective Feedback: It's All in How It's Done

For those who believe that intrinsic motivation is incompatible with negative feedback, and will ignore poor performance, the answer is that it's all in how it is done. The operative concept is constructive feedback.

The basic approach is to respect the child's dignity and competence. First, ask students to reflect on their own performance, what they did in a particular situation, how they approached a test, etc. That authentic conversation, where there is a trusting environment, will often lead to an understanding of the problem that can then be supported or refined as needed.

Next, follow with the open-ended question: *What can you/we do next time so that this will not happen the same way again?*

Giving students the first pass at corrective action deeply respects dignity and competence and does not prevent friendly and constructive adult amendment of the student's plans, along with a check-in for accountability.

## Keep Experimenting

If the open-ended question does not work, the next approach is to *give some choices* about what the student thinks might have been going on. That also respects dignity and the possibility that students are not used to being asked to self-evaluate or do not trust the open-ended approach. Those choices can be followed by the statement "Or, do you think there is something else going on?"

If neither of these works, I have found it useful to state my view of the situation as a tentative theory that requires students' response: "It looks to me as if x, y, z happened. When that happens, there are a, b, c consequences for you and others. What do you think? Am I understanding this correctly?"

The commitment to preserve the child's dignity and turn negative feedback situations into constructive feedback situations comes from the belief that it is a developmental right and necessity to nurture areas of children's competence and sense of positive possibility.

This is beyond the task of any teacher to accomplish effectively in isolation. Have conversations with your colleagues about each individual student's "day at school," and help each student have an affirming experience in school each day; this is no less important in grade 12 than it is at pre-K, or any time in between.

# Student Autonomy, Compliance, and Intrinsic Motivation

Many empirical studies have shown that excessive control from strict, negative rules and punishments and extrinsic rewards for doing the "right thing" can achieve short-term compliance.

But there are costs: it undermines intrinsic motivation, it decreases the overall quality of performance, and it connects continued performance to the availability and delivery of rewards.

This is the conundrum when education takes place in a pressured environment in which the teachers' own sense of autonomy has been eroded. Fast compliance is needed, so external controls are used which seem to "work." This success can become addictive, especially since it takes a bit of time to wean students off extrinsic rewards. It becomes seemingly easier to continue to use external controls for short-term compliance.

## Seeking Ideas from Colleagues

The solution for this is a shared philosophy and commitment to developing student autonomy in a developmentally sensitive and ongoing way—from the moment a student enters a school to the moment they depart. Everyone can't simply do their own thing; when people run into disciplinary and organizational trouble, the answer is not to revert to excessive controls. One answer is to reach out to colleagues and get ideas about how to have order and continuity while still supporting student autonomy.

## The Balance of Freedom and Order

This balance of freedom and order has been under increasing discussion of late as representing the essence of democracy and a definition of moral responsibility.

In his book, *Why We Do What We Do: Understanding Self-Motivation*, Edward Deci noted that people struggle with accepting constraints on their freedom, including having to accept some social conventions. Indeed, many societies around the world, both secular and religious, vary as to whether they place greater emphasis on freedom or order. Individuals also must find the right balance for themselves and their life situations in developmentally appropriate ways.

And this is the challenge for educators: How much freedom? How much order? The pressures of education today seem to be tilting the balance toward order and compliance, and this can have harmful long-term consequences for both children and society.

It would be foolish to advocate for autonomy at all times. Getting things done and living in social relationships with others require some structure. We have to get schools started within a time frame, move students and educators periodically, make time for nutrition and physical activity, foster creativity, and end the day in some predictable and organized ways.

The unanswered questions are: How much autonomy is enough, how much do different individuals need, and how do the answers change over time?

### Why Social-Emotional Competence and Character Matter

This has direct implications for how we present social-emotional and character development (SECD) programs, as well as programs to prevent problem behaviors. The reasons for learning SEL and having positive character are not for a grade or for rewards. SEL skills and character allow you to accomplish great things in the world.

They allow you to be helpful to others, to learn effectively, to contribute to your family, friends, school, and community, and to make your life better. These conversations must be a part of every SECD lesson.

### Addressing Risk Behaviors

Similarly, prevention of drugs, alcohol, smoking, and other tobacco and drug use, as well as violence and premature sexual behavior, needs to connect to biology, health, and relationships with others. "This is what happens to you—realistically, not in the extreme—when you engage in these actions. Here are your risks." It's essential to realize that when students feel a sense of failure, hopelessness, and lack of accomplishment, their sense of risk is different than what their teachers might think.

There is not much risk when one does not have much to lose. But when competence matters and feels attainable, behaviors that compromise that competence are easier to call into question, even in the face of peer pressure. The larger point of many of the strategies in this book is to ensure every student feels positive connection and engagement with at least some aspects of the school day.

### In Support of Classroom Autonomy

We can give Edward Deci the last word:

> At the heart of human freedom is the experience of choice. When autonomous, people experience choice about how to behave, but when controlled (whether they comply or defy), they experience a lack of choice. Intrinsic motivation represents an orientation to make choices, along with the moral compass to make responsible choices. These are attributes that only accrue positively with practice, and trust, and adults' being willing to challenge their own comfort zones toward the greater good that may result for more children when they are less controlled and more autonomous around learning. (pp. 209–210)

How do you encourage and support intrinsic motivation in your classroom and with your students?

## Nurturing Intrinsic Motivation in Students

As children come to feel effective in accomplishing something, they are more likely to try to replicate that feeling by trying to accomplish more challenging tasks. Feeling competent can be addictive. Those accomplishments are more meaningful when they are authentic, and feeling competent is itself a meaningful reward—better than a collection of stickers or small trinkets or much too scarcely distributed recognitions like "student of the month," which can lead the majority of students to become resigned to failure despite effort.

As adults, we know there is no question that extrinsic outcomes such as bonuses or promotions have instrumental value. But if they are the only definition individuals use to define their competence, those individuals are subject to a great deal of disappointment. These forms of recognition are few and far between, and relying on them, as we know from research, likely leads to declines in performance.

This is parallel to students being graded on a curve, where their own effort and competence cannot be counted on to get to a desired recognition (an A), or to being designated as student of the month in a school year in which only ten children receive that recognition. In both cases, the bar is set too high for encouragement and instead is more likely to breed unhealthy competition, cheating, jealousy, and, most often, giving up.

### Recognizing Improvement as a Form of Competence

Competence is not an absolute term. When we improve, we're becoming more competent. That's what needs to be recognized in order to encourage more improvement. One can only attain a lofty status by moving up through various levels. It's the forward movement that we must nurture.

Students intrinsically value understanding how to do more things, helping others, and feeling a sense of accomplishment at mastering new knowledge. Extrinsic reward systems often erode the latter. Think of the impact when students bring work that they're proud of to their teachers only to get a disappointing grade, or little recognition for that C+ on a test. We must nurture children's sense of accomplishment in authentic ways and provide clear feedback about how they can further improve their performance. We must be mindful not to douse a small flame just because it's not a bonfire.

The key to preserving (not creating) intrinsic motivation is to nurture students to move to the next level. This also means that in the course of the school day, children must have a chance to do things that enable them to experience accomplishment and competence instead of feeling inadequate. Many believe that children have been constructed with a lot of resilience, so that a good day does not have to mean 90 percent performance, or even 50 percent. It's not clear what the percentage is, and it may vary across children, but what is clear is that having some positive accomplishment every day will keep kids motivated to engage in school tasks.

**Intrinsic Motivation and Service Learning**
Martin Luther King, Jr. said, "Everyone can be great, because everyone can serve"—a thought that recognizes the impact and power of doing things for others. Yet service learning is under-emphasized by many schools. Students derive strong intrinsic satisfaction from helping others. Students who are struggling readers feel more confident in their reading when they help others who can learn from them, perhaps because they are younger or have a particular disability.

We can help students feel more engaged and connected to their schools by giving them roles in making the school a positive environment, such as participating in safety patrols, focusing on recycling, keeping public spaces clean, upstanding in the face of harassment and bullying, being on school committees to solve problems related to gangs or drugs and alcohol, and so on. Being contributors to their school in a positive way brings intrinsic satisfaction to students and increases their sense of competence.

**Tapping into Strengths and Interests**
Competence is propelled by curiosity and interest. Teachers need to nurture both. But as we know, education is not a solitary activity; it's a team sport. So, educators must work together to ask questions about where a given child is expressing interest,

showing curiosity, and experiencing a sense of accomplishment during every school day. For example, if a middle school student is most captivated by art class and he or she has this for only one or two quarters, the question that must be asked is: Where will the child's sense of competence be nurtured during those other quarters? Maybe that child needs to participate in an art club or otherwise be given opportunities to develop his or her artistic talents.

A quest for competence in any area can be addictive—and it's an important component of student improvement. Let's work to ensure that all students have experiences of feeling competent in school every day.

## "Do Now" Activities to Increase Student Engagement in Your Lessons

Laura Weaver and Mark Wilding, authors of *The Five Dimensions of Engaged Teaching*,[2] have identified practical examples of how educators of all grade levels might add "Do Now" activities in their classrooms to help students stay engaged or become re-engaged.

### Elementary School

*Introduce a golden moment of silence to begin the day:* A golden moment is an opportunity to sit in silence with each other as a way to quiet the body and mind. Ringing a chime or bell to mark the beginning and end of this "moment" is helpful. Teachers can encourage students to listen to the fading sound of the bell until they can no longer hear it. Teachers can start with a very short period of time—even 30 seconds—and lengthen this golden moment over time, as the students are ready and able. Use a name and rationale that makes sense to your students and fits with your current SEL and classroom routines (e.g., Calming Time, Quiet Time, Listening Minute, Settling In).

*Develop a "shared agreements" process:* In the first few weeks of school, students and teachers develop a list of agreements that will guide their classroom and define their classroom culture. These agreements co-exist alongside any school rules. Students are asked to brainstorm a list of what they need—from themselves and each other—to learn effectively, speak honestly and openly, and share what is important to them. This list is summarized in five to seven major "agreements" and posted in the classroom as a reminder. Most should be positively worded but a couple of *thou shalt not's* are fine (e.g., *no put downs*). (Examples of agreements can be found in chapter seven of Laura and Mark's book.)

## Middle School

*Have a Transitions Circle:* In the first week or two of school, engage your students in a community circle devoted to discussing the challenges and gifts of transitioning to middle school. Give each student a chance to speak for a short time (one or two minutes) on these challenges and opportunities. An alternative to this activity is to ask students to use separate index cards to anonymously write down their concerns and excitement about middle school—these can then be shared in a community circle.

In such a format, students gather into a circle and are invited to speak or share something, one by one, on a particular theme. This speaking is invitational, and no one is forced to speak. In this case, students can read one of the cards and then open it up for comments by anyone interesting in doing so. This is a non-threatening format that helps new groups of students get to know and feel comfortable with one another. If written index cards seem too early 20th century for you or your students, then consider using a shared Google document to create a community of ideas, with optional sharing and discussion to follow.

*Personalize global issues:* When including challenging topics in your lesson (such as climate change or war or a recent difficult event), give students an opportunity to share personal reactions and responses to the material. Provide ways for students to creatively express what they are seeing, feeling, and noticing in the world—past and present. One teacher follows up her lessons on climate change with an opportunity for students to create "What you can do" posters—in which students engage in brainstorms, working groups, and potential actions in their school and community.

Offering students a generative, creative, and productive outlet for the emotions that naturally get stirred by certain topics encourages learning, empowerment, and civic engagement and is intrinsically rewarding. Note: If you notice students are particularly subdued or agitated after a provocative lesson (for example, about a natural disaster or a recent tragedy), provide a few minutes for open conversation, personal response, and dialogue or ask students to reflectively write about their response to the lesson. You may wish to conclude class with quiet reflection or a lighthearted activity. If you notice extreme agitation, it is important to connect a student with other resources in the school, such as a school counselor, psychologist, or social worker.

**High School**

*Begin an occasional class with an inspirational quote or question related to your class in some way:* Ask students to engage in 3–5 minutes of reflective writing in which they respond to a quote or question. Ask for some volunteers to share out after this reflective writing. These quotes or questions can be linked to existing school, class, or unit themes, or character or SEL foci. Sir John Templeton's writings about worldwide Laws of Life and the Morning Classroom Conversations book contain excellent examples of quotes and questions that are sure to promote thinking and discussion by high school students. Some examples:

- When was the last time you were proud of yourself? In the past week, what did you do that made someone else proud—were you proud too?

- If someone followed you around the school for 30 days, what are the three words they would use to describe you? What if they followed you around outside of school? Which words would be more true about you?
- What is empathy? How do you feel when someone else shows empathy toward you? How do you know when someone is showing you empathy?
- "The secret to success is to be humble and to work hard."
- "To get joy, we must give it, and to keep joy, we must scatter it."
- "Happiness pursued eludes, happiness given returns."

*End your class with a three-to-five-minute "dyad" or "pair-share"*: Ask students to respond to a question about what one or two things they are taking with them from your class or from the school day. Have them write down a common list for their pair and submit it for your review and comment; when time allows, ask them to share with the larger group. Focus on helping students make connections between content and their lives, to help make learning relevant for them.

## All Grade Levels

*Use prospective and retrospective learning surveys:* Engage your students in age-appropriate learning goals self-reflections—in which students identify current strengths and challenges they have as learners. Ask students to identify two or three learning goals they have for this coming marking period as well as two or three learning challenges and two or three learning strengths in this class, or two or three things they feel they are best at and two or three they have the most trouble with. Take a social-emotional and academic learning approach to the surveys—in which you invite students to create goals in *each* of those areas for themselves. Let students know that you will revisit these goals mid-way through and then at the end of the marking period.

Even if you have not done this earlier in the year, at the end of the year, you can ask students to reflect on what they see as their social-emotional and academic strengths and where, in each of these areas, they feel they grew the most over this past year. And of course, you can consider the same questions for yourself.

## Notes

1 http://www.amazon.com/Why-We-What-Understanding-Self-Motivation/dp/0140255265
2 http://www.solution-tree.com/five-dimensions-engaged-teaching.html

# 9

# Educational Approach H
# Refreshing and Restoring the Soul of Educators

The Reflection/Application Guide below is designed to help you bring the ideas in each of the practice-oriented examples into your professional practice. It is meant to serve as an advanced organizer. You may want to reproduce it to have available for note-taking as you read the various practice-oriented examples.

As you are reading the practice-oriented examples linked to each approach, consider the following questions:

1. Visualize how a specific idea you are reading about might fit into your classroom/practice context.
2. Reflect on how this is similar to or different from your current practice.
3. Write three or four specific ideas you can most readily apply from the practice-oriented examples in this section.

> 4. Ask the author a question that might help to clarify, adapt, extend your understanding, etc. (SECDLab@gmail.com).

## Restoring the Soul and Skill of Educators Through Engaged Teaching

For too much of the school year, education takes a back seat to instruction. Rachael Kessler, of blessed memory, described this process two decades ago as the loss of the soul of education and, in a book of that name, spoke eloquently about how to restore it.

The needs she identified back then are even stronger now, because not only is the soul of education threatened, so are the souls of educators.

Attempting to teach children as if they are instructional units, attending inadequately to their social-emotional and character development, focusing on a select few of the multiple intelligences: these are all actions that educators know in their hearts and souls are not right. Why? Because education involves the whole child and it is possible to have high-level pedagogy, competent instruction, deep learning, and nurturing of the curiosity, intellect, hearts and souls of children and educators, all at the same time. The name given to this holistic process by Laura Weaver and Mark Wilding is "Engaged Teaching" and they describe this process in their book, *The Five Dimensions of Engaged Teaching*.[1]

I asked Laura and Mark, who consider Rachael Kessler as their primary mentor and inspiration, to share their thoughts about refreshing the soul of teachers:

*Maurice Elias: You discuss five dimensions of teaching that can lead to re-engagement and re-activation of educators' souls. What are they?*

Laura Weaver and Mark Wilding: When we think of what's right with education, we think of teachers like ourselves and the need to support our capacity as educators to reflect on and develop our own teaching practice, build productive relationships with students and colleagues, and create engaging, inclusive, and meaningful classrooms. The five dimensions of Engaged Teaching are:

1. *Cultivating an open heart:* Supports teachers to express warmth, compassion, care, and to cultivate connection with students and to build trusting, inclusive learning communities.
2. *Establishing respectful boundaries:* Supports teachers and students to develop the capacity to set limits with themselves and others and to create a safe inclusive learning community.
3. *Being present:* Supports teachers and students to bring our attention to the present moment, manage distractions, focus on the task at hand, and meaningfully engage in the learning community.
4. *Developing emotional capacity:* Supports both teachers and students to not only understand and manage their emotions, but also to expand the range of emotions that they are able to work with—both in themselves and in others.
5. *Engaging the self-observer:* Supports teachers and students to cultivate the capacity to notice, observe, and then reflect on thoughts and behaviors in order to make more conscious choices.

These dimensions are not sequential but are interrelated capacities that we cultivate simultaneously. Each of the five dimensions supports the development of the other, and together they create a whole that is more than the sum of its parts.

*Can you give us an overview of why these dimensions are important for every educator, from preschool through high school?*

The dimensions provide a framework for integrating academic, social, and emotional learning and cultural responsiveness; they also help students to connect deeply with their own sense of meaning and purpose and relevance and to connect with a diversity of peers. An Engaged Teaching framework is not an add-on program or curriculum, but rather an integrated approach to teaching and learning for any grade level or content area. It is really about capacity building: supporting educators in sustainably integrating social, emotional, and academic learning in their classrooms and to build healthy and vibrant learning communities with their students and colleagues.

*How are these dimensions essential for true academic learning?*

Together, the five dimensions nourish and support the development of the whole student—healthy heart, mind, and inner life—that we feel is the foundation of academic learning. Each of the dimensions supports students to foster meaningful connections to themselves, each other, their schoolwork, and their world. The approach supports students to learn to honor difference, observe their own thoughts and behaviors, manage distractions and emotions, more effectively focus on schoolwork, think critically and creatively, and discover more about themselves and one another. When students are given these opportunities, they are more able and motivated to engage deeply in school, develop resilience, and act compassionately. When students feel safe and supported, when they feel valued and known, when they are given opportunities to express their authentic selves, and when they are given the skills to communicate effectively and focus well, they are truly ready and able to learn and to contribute in positive ways to the world around them.

## Like a Flourishing Tree

Laura and Mark use the analogy of a tree to show how Engaged Teaching is relevant to aspiring, new, and veteran educators, much as a forest needs healthy, growing seedlings, saplings, and young and mature trees. The roots of the tree, that nurture and inform the trunk of the tree (consisting of the five dimensions described earlier), are:

- Addressing developmental stages;
- Fostering connection, meaning, and purpose;
- Responding to cultural contexts;
- Investing in relationships and community; and
- Social, emotional, and academic learning.

The resulting flourishing branches include proximal outcomes such as improved classroom climate, student attitudes toward learning, collaboration, and social-emotional skills. With continued nurturing, these branches eventually flower into improved student academic performance, behavior, and school climate. It's seeing our students flourish—despite challenges and hassles—that fosters restoration of the soul of educators and your pride and joy in your work.

## The Hardest Job in America

The hardest job in America? Being a teacher, so said Sargent Shriver[2] on October 13, 1972, in a speech given as part of his vice-presidential campaign with George McGovern. Over half a century after this remarkable speech, his words bear sharing.

Sargent Shriver begins by saying that it is the hardest job "not just because the teachers of America have been blamed and castigated for all the ills" of our educational system. The fact is that teachers are not the causes of these ills but are victims themselves, "not just because teachers often work in archaic schools with inadequate facilities for both teacher and child," and "not just because a narrow officialdom has bogged teachers down in massive red tape wasteful of time and destructive of initiative" (did Sarge ever have to do student growth objectives, I wonder?), and that all of these, and more, are "difficult, frustrating obstacles in your profession."

Shriver says that it's the hardest job because teachers are expected to teach students values that they are not seeing lived all around them and in the society overall. What are the values that Shriver believes are central to effective education? They are not controversial: reverence for life, honesty and truth, brotherhood/sisterhood and unity, and desire and respect for knowledge and education.

Why did Shriver believe these values were not a priority to educational policymakers and not first in the minds of children? Four reasons, each one as relevant today as in 1972:

1. Much more money is spent on war than on education.
2. Hungry, sick, and uncared for children are not a priority of the federal government. "This Administration doesn't even seem to comprehend that those problems are all handicaps to a child's education."
3. Our national, state, and local politicians and educational leaders do not model these essential values.
4. Too many communities in which many of our children live, which surround the schools, are characterized by poor housing and recreation, inadequate health care, joblessness, racial/ethnic discrimination, and hopelessness, which "all find their way to the school door. A child who is hungry, or sleepy or sick or on drugs cannot learn."

I hope you are as struck as I am by how Shriver's words from 1972 resonate in the present. He was not being prescient. He was describing his situation at the time with brutal honesty. He could not have known, and likely could not have imagined, that the conditions he spoke about would largely persist over five decades later.

## What Did Shriver Recommend?
The context of the speech, of course, gives you Shriver's ultimate recommendation: Elect George McGovern to the White House and he would create the changes needed, with Shriver's assistance.

But we need something a bit more contemporary, and from the speech, we can extract three of Shriver's ideas that we can apply to the present:

1. *Provide early childhood education.* This ensures that especially disadvantaged youth have a "head start" that allows them to begin school less far behind. Shriver was not just advocating universal preschool. He wanted children to have the health and dental care of the Head Start program, and he wanted their parents to have education, parenting support, and job and housing assistance.

2. *Create political coalitions to raise voices on behalf of those who do not have a political voice.* Persistent, strong leadership in the cause of children's well-being is what creates political momentum. Shriver knew this from his prior successes in the War on Poverty and the expansion of the Head Start program.

3. *Make schools places where the essential values are lived.* Let children see, day in and day out, what it means to come every day for over half a year to a place where life is revered, honesty and truth are cherished, knowledge and education are respected, and the diverse adults and children in and around the building involved with education experience unity.

There is a lot in Shriver's speech that was rooted in the politics of 1972, but there is much more that is rooted in enduring reality. The impossible conditions that so many teachers labor under, as enumerated by Shriver, as debilitating as they are, do not carry the emotional and personal weight of trying to get children to follow a path not lived around them.

So, while we look to political and policy action to correct the larger systemic problems, let's look within and make our schools places that nurture children's social-emotional and character development in the best possible ways.

When the school doors are open, and everyone is eager to enter and looks forward to returning the next day, we will have taken major steps to making the hardest job in America less difficult, and far more rewarding.

## Notes

1 http://www.solution-tree.com/five-dimensions-engaged-teaching.html
2 http://en.wikipedia.org/wiki/Sargent_Shriver

# Conclusion

You have journeyed through practice-based examples of eight educational approaches that might not seem, on the surface, to be "educational approaches." In part, this could be because the premise of educational engagement in this book is that students are led by their hearts—their emotions and passions—more than by their minds. Of course, ultimately, heart, head, and hand all must be engaged for deep, accessible learning. And learning is something that can be inspired and ignited in students—most often through their emotions. Students respond when something "happens" to them in the learning situation. They feel some personal, affective connection to what is occurring in the classroom or other part of the school. It's deeply personal. That's why this book has prioritized ways to create a learning environment in which all students can thrive.

There is no single best way to accomplish this. Not all students will respond to the same approaches. We, as educators, are not equally comfortable with and confident in our ability to excel at all approaches. The eight approaches presented here allow many ways "in" to the soul of students. We can directly focus on classroom and school culture, as recommended in approaches A and B. We may find our students respond to encouraging their strengths and growth mindset, through the examples in approach C. Particularly at the secondary level, our students may benefit from sources of inspiration and human dignity, and appreciate the opportunity to articulate their most strongly held values and sense of positive purpose. For these students, approaches D and E will yield useful examples.

Our classrooms and schools all benefit when our students develop an attitude of gratitude and become more aware of and thankful for many of the things in their lives that they perhaps have taken for granted. Doing this via approach F often opens the door to intrinsic motivation, approach G. There is no doubt that in a society of instant gratification and frequent "rewards" and "likes," educators need to pay explicit attention to cultivating intrinsic motivation. Of course, intrinsic motivation already exists. Our challenge is to allow it to come to the fore amidst many educational systems and approaches that focus on tangible rewards to keep students on task.

I invoked Rachael Kessler and Sargent Shriver to remind us of the need for educators to take care of themselves and one another. Foremost is to realize that teaching and organizing schools for social, emotional, and academic development and multiple literacies is work of tremendous importance. This is not typically recognized in salary structures, public respect, parental approval, or working conditions. Ultimately, it is intrinsic motivation that keeps educators going, and we need to say to ourselves how hard and essential the job is, and we need to share and state this appreciation to our colleagues. Approach H—educator refreshment, renewal, and spiritual nurturing—requires constant attention. It's not immodest to have this focus, any more than it is to recharge batteries regularly.

Through daily repetition of some of these approaches and the practice-based examples that embody them, we can make significant inroads into inspiring learning and social-emotional competence and character in our students, and recommit ourselves to the importance of our jobs. Onward!

# Bibliography

Ahmed, S. (2025, February 2). In Gaza, we cannot look away. *New York Times*, SR 6–7. https://www.nytimes.com/2025/02/02/opinion/gaza-israel-cease-fire-hope.html

Anderson, J., & Winthrop, R. (2025, January 4). Giving kids autonomy has surprising results. *New York Times*, A19. https://www.nytimes.com/2025/01/02/opinion/children-choices-goal-setting.html

Brackett, M. (2020). *Permission to feel*. Celadon Books.

Brooks, A., & Dalai Lama (2016, November 4). Arthur Brooks and the Dalai Lama: Behind our anxiety, the fear of being unneeded. *New York Times*. http://nyti.ms/2e7B49O

Brooks, D. (2025, January 10). The character-building tool kit. *New York Times*, A22. https://www.nytimes.com/2025/01/09/opinion/character-building-education.html

Cantor, P. (2021). All children thriving: A new purpose for education. *American Educator*, 45(3), 14–26, 48.

Cedano, S. M., Tavarez, Y., Elias, M. J., & MacDonnell, M. (2022). Building socially engaged classrooms: How Students Taking Action Together (STAT) helps facilitate conversations around contemporary issues for youth's civic action. *Children & Schools*, 44(2), 116–119. https://doi.org/10.1093/cs/cdab033

Cipriano, C. et al. (2023). The state of evidence for social and emotional learning: A contemporary meta-analysis of universal school-based SEL interventions. *Child Development*, 94(5), 1181–1204. https://doi.org/10.1111/cdev

Cipriano, C., Naples, L. H., Eveleigh, A., Cook, A., Funaro, M., Cassidy, C., McCarthy, M. F., & Rappolt-Schlichtmann, G. (2023). A systematic review of student disability and race representation in universal school-based social and emotional learning interventions for elementary school students. *Review of Educational Research,* 93(1), 73–102. https://doi.org/10.3102/00346543221094079

Consortium on the School-Based Promotion of Social Competence (Elias, Weissberg, Dodge, Hawkins, Kendall, Jason, Perry, Rotheram, & Zins). (1991). Preparing students for the twenty-first century: Contributions of the prevention and social competence promotion fields. *Teachers College Record, 93,* 97–105.

Damon, W., Menon, J., & Cotton Bronk, K. (2003). The development of purpose during adolescence. *Applied Developmental Science, 7,* 119–128.

Davidson, M., Lickona, T., & Khmelkov, V. (2014). Smart & good schools: A new paradigm for high school education. In L. Nucci, D. Narvaez, & T. Krettenauer (Eds.), *Handbook of moral and character education* (2nd ed.) (pp. 290–307). Taylor and Francis.

Douthat, R. (2025, May 11). Chris Murphy still thinks that Democrats are still in denial. *New York Times,* SR 6. https://www.nytimes.com/2025/05/08/opinion/democrats-working-class-chris-murphy.html

Durlak, J. A., Weissberg, R. P., Dymnicki, A. B., Taylor, R. D., & Schellinger, K. B. (2011). The impact of enhancing students' social and emotional learning: A meta-analysis of school-based universal interventions. *Child Development, 82*(1), 405–432. https://doi.org/10.1111/j.1467-8624.2010.01564.x

Elbot, C. F., & Fulton, D. V. (2007). *Building an intentional school culture.* Corwin Press.

Elias, M. J. (Ed.) (2013). Promoting students' social-emotional and character development and preventing bullying. Special issue of the *Korean Journal of Educational Policy, 10*(3).

Elias, M. J., & Leverett, L. (2011). Consultation to urban schools for improvements in academics and behavior: No alibis. No excuses. No exceptions. *Journal of Educational and Psychological Consultation, 21,* 1–17.

Elias, M. J., & Leverett, L. (2021). *Addressing equity through culturally responsive education and SEL.* National Professional Resources, Inc.

Elias, M. J., Murphy, N., & McClain, K. (2022). *Morning classroom conversations: Build your students' social-emotional, character and communication skills every day*. Corwin.

Frankl, V. (1959). *Man's search for meaning: An introduction to logotherapy*. Beacon.

Fullmer, L., Bond, L., Nayman, S., Molyneaux, C., & Elias, M. J. (2022). *Students taking action together: 5 teaching techniques to cultivate SEL, civic engagement, and a healthy democracy*. ASCD.

Gager, P. J., & Elias, M. J. (1997). Implementing prevention programs in high risk environments: Application of the resiliency paradigm. *American Journal of Orthopsychiatry, 67*(3), 363–373.

Ginwright, S. (2018, May 31). The future of healing: Shifting from trauma informed care to healing centered engagement. *Medium*. https://medium.com/@ginwright/the-future-ofhealing-shifting-from-trauma-informed-care-to-healing-centered-engagement-634f557ce69c

Hatchimonji, D. R., Vaid, E., Linsky, A. C. V., & Nayman, S. J. (2022). Exploring relations among social-emotional and character development targets: Character virtue, social-emotional learning skills, and positive purpose. *International Journal of Emotional Education, 14*(1), 20–37. https://doi.org/10.56300/EVIP7836

Hung, C., Ni, Y., Geldhof, G. J., Berg, J., & McMahon, R. (2023). Life goal selection pattern and purpose in adolescence: A latent class analysis. *Journal of Adolescence, 95*(7), 1365–1376. https://doi.org/10.1002/jad.12209

Kress, J. E., & Elias, M. J. (2020). *Nurturing students' character: Everyday teaching activities for social-emotional learning*. Routledge. (Translated into Greek and Chinese.)

Mahoney, J., Domitrovich, C., & Durlak, J. (Eds.) (2025). *Handbook of social and emotional learning* (2nd ed.). Guilford.

Malin, H. (2018). *Teaching for purpose: Preparing students for lives of meaning*. Harvard Education Press.

McCaulley, E. (2025, January 20). The day calls for Marin Luther King's vision. *New York Times*, A20. https://www.nytimes.com/2025/01/20/opinion/martin-luther-king-trump.html

Minian, A. R. (2025). America has not lived up to its promise. *New York Times*, A18. https://www.nytimes.com/2025/01/22/opinion/trump-immigrants-deportations.html

Nayman, S. J., Elias, M. J., Selby, E. A., Fishman, D. B., Linsky, A. C. V., & Hatchimonji, D. R. (2019). The relationship among purpose classification, purpose engagement, and purpose commitment in low socioeconomic status and ethnically diverse adolescents. *Journal of Character Education, 15*(2), 53–70.

Noguera, P., Cammarota, J., & Ginwright, J. (2013). *Beyond resistance! Youth activism and community change*. Routledge.

Osher, D. et al. (2020). Drivers of human development: How relationships and context shape learning and development. *Applied Developmental Science 24*(1), 6–36. https://doi.org/10.1080/10888691.2017.1398650

Pawlo, E., Lorenzo, A., Eichert, B., & Elias, M. J. (2019). All SEL should be trauma-informed. *Phi Delta Kappan, 101*(3), 37–41. https://doi.org/10.1177/0031721719885919

Poedubicky, V., & Elias, M. J. (2021). *Social-emotional learning lab: A comprehensive SEL resource kit*. Research Press.

Rimm-Kaufman, S. E. (2021). *SEL from the start*. W. W. Norton.

Rimm-Kaufman, S. E., Strambler, M. J., & Schonert-Reichl, K. A. (2023). *Social and emotional learning in action: Creating systemic change in schools*. Guilford Press.

Sarason, S. B. (1982). *The culture of the school and the problem of change* (2nd ed.). Allyn & Bacon.

Yuan, M., MacDonnell, M., Poliakova, P., Hatchimonji, D., Linsky, A., & Elias, M. J. (2025). Testing the social-emotional and character development (SECD) approach with student mental health and academic outcomes. *Social and Emotional Learning: Research, Practice, and Policy, 5*, 100105, https://doi.org/10.1016/j.sel.2025.100105

## Blog Bibliography

https://www.edutopia.org/blog/4-approaches-building-positive-community-any-classroom-maurice-elias

https://www.edutopia.org/article/important-questions-ask-your-students

https://www.edutopia.org/blog/students-create-end-of-year-legacy-now-maurice-elias

https://www.edutopia.org/blog/school-spirit-discipline-sel-maurice-elias

https://www.edutopia.org/blog/positive-climate-culture-inclusive-schools-promote-sel-maurice-elias

https://www.edutopia.org/blog/improving-class-climate-improves-class-climate-maurice-elias

https://www.edutopia.org/blog/socially-inclusive-school-benefits-everyone-maurice-elias

https://www.edutopia.org/article/two-step-process-reducing-chronic-absenteeism

https://www.edutopia.org/blog/you-need-elevator-pitch-about-school-culture-and-climate-maurice-elias

https://www.edutopia.org/article/evaluating-school-culture-climate

https://www.edutopia.org/blog/feelings-walking-tour-surveying-school-climate-maurice-elias

https://www.edutopia.org/article/sel-walls-school

https://www.edutopia.org/blog/what-kind-ecosystem-your-school-maurice-elias

https://www.edutopia.org/blog/guide-your-students-toward-positive-fulfillment-maurice-elias

https://www.edutopia.org/blog/students-strengths-passions-maurice-elias

https://www.edutopia.org/article/framework-student-goal-setting

https://www.edutopia.org/blog/building-positive-mindset-one-word-time-maurice-elias

https://www.edutopia.org/blog/teaching-moment-peace-corps-anniversary-maurice-elias

https://www.edutopia.org/article/helping-students-respectfully-disagree

https://www.edutopia.org/blog/maya-angelou-poetry-lesson-sel-maurice-elias

https://www.edutopia.org/blog/lesson-about-cesar-chavez-civil-rights-maurice-elias

https://www.edutopia.org/blog/liberty-bell-history-students-should-know-pbl-maurice-elias

https://www.edutopia.org/blog/helping-your-students-identify-their-values-maurice-elias

https://www.edutopia.org/blog/guiding-students-finding-their-truth-maurice-elias

https://www.edutopia.org/blog/helping-students-find-purpose-and-appreciation-school-maurice-elias

https://www.edutopia.org/article/developing-sense-purpose-school

https://www.edutopia.org/blog/heart-habits-gratitude-students-reflect-act-on-maurice-elias

https://www.edutopia.org/blog/forgiveness-gratitude-lessons-sel-maurice-elias

https://www.edutopia.org/blog/gratitude-builds-health-character-maurice-elias

https://www.edutopia.org/blog/strategies-teaching-holidays-december-maurice-elias

https://www.edutopia.org/blog/how-and-why-intrinsic-motivation-works-maurice-elias

https://www.edutopia.org/blog/student-autonomy-compliance-and-intrinsic-motivation-maurice-elias

https://www.edutopia.org/article/nurturing-intrinsic-motivation-students

https://www.edutopia.org/blog/engaged-teaching-do-now-activities-sel-lessons-maurice-elias

https://www.edutopia.org/blog/soul-skill-restoring-engaged-teaching-sel-maurice-elias

https://www.edutopia.org/blog/hardest-job-america-teaching-maurice-elias

For Product Safety Concerns and Information please contact our EU
representative  GPSR@taylorandfrancis.com
Taylor & Francis Verlag GmbH, Kaufingerstraße 24, 80331 München, Germany

www.ingramcontent.com/pod-product-compliance
Lightning Source LLC
Chambersburg PA
CBHW052341230426
43664CB00041B/2608